The MEDIEVAL UNIVERSITY

The
MEDIEVAL
UNIVERSITY
1200-1400

Lowrie J. Daly, S.J.
SAINT LOUIS UNIVERSITY

with an Introduction by
Pearl Kibre

SHEED AND WARD — NEW YORK

© SHEED & WARD, INC., 1961

LIBRARY OF CONGRESS CATALOG CARD NUMBER 61–11787

MANUFACTURED IN THE UNITED STATES OF AMERICA

To My Mother

TO THE READER

This volume is intended for college students and teachers who in the course of their work have need of a summary of information about medieval universities. For this reason footnotes have been omitted, materials have been synopsized from the standard works in the field, and exemplary documents have been added.

CONTENTS

CONTENTS

INTRODUCTION

The provision of a means for the education of large numbers of persons through the organized curricula of monastic, abbey, and cathedral schools, and eventually of the university associations, is one of the remarkable achievements of the Middle Ages. It is an accomplishment for which the modern world might justly be grateful. The aim of making available the elements of learning to all who had the ability and the will to learn, already expressed in the capitularies of Charlemagne at the close of the eighth century, might well be compared to the modern democratic ideal of providing educational opportunities for all. Moreover, the stimulus, encouragement, and active assistance provided by leading potentates, ecclesiastical as well as lay, throughout the Middle Ages, for the attainment of this goal, might also provide an inspiring example for modern administrators and legislators.

In the light of the above, it is significant that there has recently been manifest an upsurge of interest in the educational developments of the medieval period. However, such concern following the ground-breaking labors of the nineteenth-century giants in the field, Father Heinrich Denifle and Hastings Rashdall, has been confined to a comparatively small coterie of scholars. Their specialized works have for the most part left the general reader and the student beginning his work in the field hopelessly at sea. Thus it had become increasingly evident that an introductory study was needed to provide a bridge between the scholarly monographs and the interests of the non-specialist in the field.

One may therefore rejoice that this need has now been met by so eminent a scholar in the field of medieval studies as Father Lowrie J. Daly. His study of the medieval university has anticipated the perplexities that beset the student unfamiliar with the field by providing a general introduction to the entire subject. He has thus brought together the principal threads of development leading to the university association. And he has treated not only of the organization and administration of the latter but also of the nature, content, and preparation of the materials taught. To illustrate these points, Father Daly has made frequent references to the documents translated by Professor Lynn Thorndike, and he has appended a number of them to his study. At the close of each section, Father Daly has further provided a carefully selected bibliography of pertinent works to which the interested student or reader can turn for more specialized treatment of any given phase of the subject. The present work therefore not only provides an introductory overview of the field for the student or non-specialist, it also affords the scholar an opportunity to have at hand a convenient guide to the recent monographic literature on various phases of university development.

PEARL KIBRE
HUNTER COLLEGE

I. FROM CLOISTER WALLS TO
UNIVERSITY HALLS

In any essay on the medieval universities, something must be said of the intellectual and the educational backgrounds. Before describing briefly two main agencies of higher schooling (the monastic and the cathedral schools), it is important to note the problems which faced the medieval educators. Unless their difficulties are understood, the value of their accomplishment will not be fully appreciated.

OBSTACLES TO EDUCATION DURING
EARLY MEDIEVAL TIMES

One of the quickest ways to judge of the influence and strength of any educational system is to investigate the qualifications of its teachers. An obvious thing about the educational history of Europe from the seventh to the twelfth century is that, generally speaking, whatever education there was, was due to the Church and her clerics. Consequently, the gradual encroachment of feudalism on the administrative life of the Church and the increasing control by laymen of Church properties and appointments from the early ninth to the middle of the eleventh century had in many ways a bad effect on education. Although many dukes and lords established and en-

1

dowed monasteries and many sent their sons to the monastic "extern" schools, still their greedy seizure of choice bishoprics and abbacies, their intrusion into ecclesiastical administration of men fitted neither by education nor ideals for spiritual duties, inevitably had its effect on the clerical body. Owing to the circumstances of the times, a lay lord often selected one of his serfs, saw to it that he got the barest essentials of a theological training, and then put him into the local parish church on his estate. This did not tend to raise the educational standards of the neighboring countryside very much. As the coarseness of the times spread, it weakened education because it vitally sapped the strength of the clergy, who were the educators of the time. The stern fight of Gregory VII (1073–1085) to break secular control of ecclesiastical appointments and to reform the lives of the clergy was of great importance in the history of education because it connoted an improvement in the quality and training of the medieval educators.

Another great obstacle to the progress of education was the political situation. Europe during the ninth and tenth centuries has been compared to a besieged fortress. It was attacked on the south by the Moslems, who ravaged the coasts of Italy—pillaging, for example, the great basilica of St. Peter's in 846; by the Hungarians from the East, who carried fire and sword through the lands of eastern Germany; by the terrible Vikings, or Northmen, who destroyed monasteries and towns in Ireland, England, and France. The Northmen were especially dreaded because with their long narrow boats, capable of navigating both rivers and seas, they possessed a naval mobility and striking power that had no equal in the Europe of their day. Imbued with a bitter hatred of things Christian, the

2

Northmen delighted in destroying the monasteries and their libraries. Modern people have experienced the bitter destructions of two terrible wars; but, until recently, our ability to rebuild has been on a par with our power to destroy. The sad plight of our ninth- and tenth-century ancestors was that they could not reconstruct nearly so easily. Furthermore, the havoc wrought was so frequent and systematic that it brought apathy and discouragement. The total effect was a wholesale diminution both of the places where learning had taken refuge and of the only groups of people who possessed it.

Another obstacle, familiar to all teachers in some degree, was the lack of interest in education. The average worker of Europe was a farmer. The seven liberal arts and a "college education" were of little practical value to him. As a matter of fact, few people of those times really needed the type of literary training which forms the core of higher education. Printing was far in the future; and books, in comparison with their numbers in modern times, were relatively scarce and expensive. Newspapers and magazines did not exist. To many persons of that era higher education did not seem as necessary as the knowledge of how to plant and harvest and follow the agricultural routine. And since the average European did not find that proficiency in scholastic subjects usually meant an increase of income, the subject of higher education remained of purely academic interest.

A final obstacle was the dearth of "physical equipment." A modern teacher takes for granted such items as adequate lighting, paper and pen, sufficient and accurately printed texts and reference books. Note-taking, too, was a relatively more difficult process in those days. Although textbooks were not

3

as frequently changed as is the modern practice, they were relatively more expensive. It might require six or eight months of a scribe's labor to reproduce a single large work. Although monasteries and schools, including the universities, had systems for copying books, it would seem that the price of books still remained a serious deterrent in some instances. The relatively small number of volumes in medieval libraries seems to give additional evidence of this.

In the light of these various obstacles the difficulty of the medieval teachers is more readily understood and the value of their effective teaching more highly esteemed. There were no great state-supported educational systems, nor even solitary schools. Practically speaking, the Church was the only institution in Europe that showed consistent interest in the preservation and cultivation of knowledge.

One advantage which the medieval teacher had over his modern counterpart was an international language, Latin, which could be used as a standard medium of communication of thought anywhere in Europe among educated people. Its benefits were strikingly manifested when the universities began to develop, although even during the earlier period the possession of such a common language was something any modern university teacher might envy. Latin was the language of lawyers, of diplomats, of educators. When a nobleman made his last will and testament, for example, he made it in Latin. In the age of the universities, when a student wrote home to his father about the sad state of his exchequer, Latin was the language he used, even though he probably found himself a scribe versed in the art of letter-writing, an art "often and

4

exceeding necessary for the clergy, for monks suitable and for laymen honorable."

For this period in medieval educational history, and well on into the formative period of the universities, *the teacher was the school*. Students sought out the great and famous teachers and studied under them, much as is done by graduate students in certain fields today. There were, however, two general types of "schools" or places where instruction was customarily given. Both of them were organizational units in the life of the Church. These were the monastic and the cathedral schools.

THE MONASTIC AND CATHEDRAL SCHOOLS

Until the year 1100 or thereabouts, it seems that a very large percentage of the places concerned with the business of learning and education were connected with monasteries. It has been well said that during much of the earlier period education was really monasticism. In specialized discussions regarding the exact meaning of the rule of St. Benedict (480–545), it has been pointed out that either the idea that monks were agricultural specialists or that all of them studied and taught would have been equally surprising to St. Benedict. The early Benedictine monk was certainly not a scholar like the Maurists, nor did he perform as much agricultural work as some modern Trappists do. But it can certainly be said that the average monk did read and study a great deal. More than this, when applicants were received into the monastery, a certain amount of education had to be provided. Some novices had to be taught to

5

read Latin sufficiently well to perform choir duties, to make spiritual reading, and perhaps to copy manuscripts, for this last was a common exercise in many monasteries. By reason of these necessities schools developed in many monasteries in Europe. Primarily designed for the education of the applicants to the monastic way of life, these schools frequently enrolled the sons of local nobility. Such a group of extern students, not intending to become monks but coming merely for schooling, caused problems for some monastic legislators. Benedict of Aniane, a great monastic legislator, did not think it a wise procedure, and in 817 through his influence, orders were issued at Aachen forbidding monasteries to admit lay students to their schools. How effective this kind of legislation was is hard to estimate. At least one result was the establishment of "outer" schools; that is, schools which were outside the monastery proper. But it would seem that these schools for "externs" were a hardy growth and continued in many monasteries during the period, regardless of some monastic legislators; often, too, the local abbot might have very different ideas about the usefulness of such work for his monks and its connection with their sanctification.

Monastic schools continued all through the early Middle Ages, and it was not until the rise of the universities in the twelfth and thirteenth centuries that they began to take second place and gradually lost their educational influence. Their curriculum was literary and somewhat static, and they took little or no part in the great philosophical and theological movements. Monastic education, after the rise of the universities, tended to become a "private possession." In the later Middle Ages some of the monasteries, with the firm encouragement of the papacy, attempted to open branch houses at some of the universities, but the program was not successful, and the educational leadership passed into other hands.

The cathedral, or "bishop's," school was, as the name implies, a school established by the bishop, taught by his own clergy either in his own house or in a place nearby, and intended primarily to train future priests for his own diocese. Today these would be called diocesan seminaries; they were in existence in greater or less number, depending upon the local conditions. The cathedral schools reached their greatest development in the late eleventh and the early twelfth centuries, and some of them later grew into universities. Most of the cathedral schools, after the rise of the universities, tended to stress philosophy and theology, although there were exceptions which laid greater stress on literature—as, for example, Orleans and Chartres. In general, the monastic schools tended to become the places for literary studies, while the cathedral schools followed the "more modern" fashion of stressing the new philosophical and theological trends.

The ecclesiastical attitude toward the progress of knowledge was put in permanent form by the decree of the Third Lateran Council in 1179:

Since the church of God as a kindly mother is held to provide for those needs which pertain to physical welfare and those which contribute to the progress of souls, lest the opportunity of reading and education be denied poor children who cannot be aided by the resources of their parents, let some sufficient benefice be set aside in every cathedral church for a master who shall teach the clergy of the same church and poor scholars gratis, whereby the need for a teacher shall be met and the way to knowledge opened to learners.

7

In other churches, too, and monasteries, if in time past any provision has been made for this purpose, let it be re-established. And for the permission to teach let no one demand any fee whatever, or ask anything from teachers under the cover of some custom, or forbid any fit person to teach if he seeks permission. Moreover, whoever presumes to contravene this, let him be deprived of ecclesiastical benefice, since he seems to deserve deprivation of the fruits of his labor in the church of God who from cupidity of mind, while he sells the license to teach, strives to impede the progress of the church.[1]

SUBJECTS FOR STUDY

The curriculum of early medieval education was composed of the seven liberal arts. They were "liberal" arts or studies because they were considered to be especially fitting to the "free" (*liberi*) men in distinction to those who were lower in the social scale, and they were the usual subjects of higher studies in the early Middle Ages. These seven liberal arts were subdivided in the "three" (*trivium*) of grammar, rhetoric, and dialectic, and the "four" (*quadrivium*) of arithmetic, geometry, astronomy, and music.

Their content was not quite what their name suggests today. Grammar meant Latin grammar, but it included facility in speaking and writing and dealt with Latin literature as well as grammar rules. Rhetoric was the study of the "art of speaking well on civil questions"—in Latin, of course. One recognizes

[1] Reprinted with permission from Lynn Thorndike, *University Records and Life in the Middle Ages* (New York: Columbia University Press, 1944), p. 10.

8

immediately the carry-over from Roman times and the ideal *eloquentia* of the rhetoricians. Medieval rhetoric tended to emphasize letter-writing ability, which itself gradually developed into an art, the *ars dictaminis*. Dialectic was the study of reasoning skills in some ways comparable to logic courses in a modern arts faculty. Arithmetic concerned simple calculations and aided in determining the movable date of Easter. Incidentally, Roman numbers and not Arabic ones were in use, and multiplication with the Roman type was not easy. Try, for example, 608 x 75—i.e., DCVIII x LXXV! In geometry class the student learned something about geography and surveying, but modern geometry dates from about the twelfth century, when translations of Arabic books, themselves translations from Greek, became available. Astronomy was a study of the stars, sometimes cluttered up with astrology. Centuries before, St. Augustine had devoted a considerable part of the fifth book of his *City of God* to demolishing the astrologers. Despite his criticisms, astrologers and fortune-tellers seemed a perennial phenomenon. Music, the last of the liberal arts, was more theoretical and mathematical than what is generally connoted by the term today.

Bishop Gregory of Tours (538–593) thus described the seven arts in his *History of the Franks:*

... Our Martianus has taught you the seven arts, that is ... by means of grammar he has taught you how to read, through dialectic to discuss statements for debate, through rhetoric to know the kinds of verse, through geometry to figure the measurements for planes and lines, by astronomy to study the courses of the stars, through arithmetic to determine the characteristics of numbers, and through music to harmonize different tones in songs of pleasing accent. . . .

During the twelfth century educational interests began to change with the rise of the dialectical method in theology. The first experiments were not entirely successful. Indeed many scholars believed the method did more harm than good. On one side were the ascetical writers, and for most of them, from St. Peter Damian in the time of Lanfranc to St. Bernard in the time of Abelard, the attitude was much the same: this type of study was a menace to the Faith, what the Church taught was enough; Catholics should simply accept whatever difficulties might be involved in the intellectual content of the Faith, there should be no further attempt to resolve them, and so forth. As a matter of fact, the attempts of the new theological dialecticians to put their theories into practice seemed almost to prove the conservative position. In the explanations of an outstanding proponent of the new methods, Abelard, the Trinity of Persons in God seemed to be merely God's Power, Wisdom, and Love; original sin appeared impossible; and the humanity of Christ seemed to be joined to the Divinity in a union that was no more than moral—all this running counter to the clear teaching of the Church. And in the books written at Chartres, a center of philosophical studies, Neoplatonic tendencies toward pantheism seemed evident.

St. Bernard and Abelard were two of the great personalities of the twelfth century. They were often on opposite sides of a controversy. St. Bernard was convinced that Abelard summed up in his own person all the dangerous tendencies of these new dialectical theologians, who appeared to him to be cluttering up the intellectual landscape and seriously trespassing on the domains of Faith.

Abelard, indeed, was probably his own worst enemy. Undoubtedly a vain man, he was also undoubtedly a very brilliant scholar, who dearly loved a quarrel. An inveterate dialectician, he was also one of the greatest teachers that ever graced the classroom. In his *Sic et Non* ("Yes and No") he started a movement in theology which reached perfection in the production of the great *Summa* of St. Thomas and continued in the traditions of scholasticism, of using the tools of reason and its syllogisms to work out answers in matters of revelation. Basically what Abelard did was to gather opinions of various early theologians, principally Fathers of the Church like Augustine, Leo, Hilary, as well as materials from the Scriptures. He set side by side judgments which seemed at first view contradictory. It was then up to reason to work out a solution. Since Truth cannot be at variance with Itself, and the truths of both reason and revelation are from the same God, there must be a slip in the reasoning or a mistake in the theological citation, in a given case where the authorities are actually in conflict. This method, seen in its perfection in the objections, solution to the question, and answers to the objections which fill the pages of St. Thomas' *Summa*, was a very stimulating one. It was also a very disquieting one to those conservative minds who did not yet see clearly that reason was going to be on the side of revelation. Furthermore, Abelard's own rashness incurred for him a batch of dogmatic errors regarding the Trinity, the redemption, and original sin which his enemies were not slow to ex-

11

ploit. Abelard was never a rationalist, if by that term is meant one who denies such things as revelation, miracles, or the Catholic Faith. He wrote to Héloise: "I have no desire to be a philosopher in contradiction to St. Paul nor an Aristotle separated from Christ, for there is no other name under heaven in which I can be saved. . . . The rock on which I have built my knowledge is that on which Christ has built his Church."

Unquestionably Abelard and other famous teachers drew thousands of students to their classrooms, and this gave great impetus to the movement which culminated in the creation of the medieval universities. But Abelard was not the only educator of the twelfth century; nor was it only the use of dialectics in theology which drew criticism. There were also teachers at variance with the older literary and classical traditions of higher education, and the emphasis on dialectics to the exclusion of the other liberal arts raised up opponents among groups other than the conservative theologians. One of the most outspoken critics in some matters of the new emphasis on dialectics, as well as one of our best sources for the educational picture before the formation of the universities, was John of Salisbury. The career of this man, one of the best-educated of medieval scholars, was a varied one.

JOHN OF SALISBURY (ABOUT 1125–1180)

John was a native of the old medieval town of Salisbury which is today known as Old Sarum. As a small boy he had been sent to a certain priest to be instructed in his *Psalter*, the book of Psalms, but the priest seems to have been more interested in crystal-gazing than in education, as John's account, given in his *Polycraticus*, indicates. John adds that he never knew anyone who followed such practices who came to a happy end of life except two, and one of them was this master.[2]

Some time between the Christmas of 1135 and that of 1136, John went to France to continue his studies. He was a student of the "Peripatetic of Pallet," as John called Abelard, for about a year, then of Alberic, next of Robert of Melun, and finally of William, the grammarian of Conches, who was for a time the tutor of Henry II. After this he spent some three years at the famous school of Chartres, little dreaming, probably, that he was to be the bishop of that city forty years later. Here he studied grammar, in the wide medieval meaning of the subject, and also rhetoric, with Theodoric (or Thierry) of Chartres, as well as some of the subjects of the *quadrivium*. He also seems to have met Gilbert de la Porrée while at Chartres. About the year 1140 John apparently returned to Paris to continue his studies under Peter Helias, a commentator on the grammarian Priscian, and with the Aristotelian Adam du Petit Pont, Gilbert de la Porrée (whom he had for theology and logic), Robert Pullus (or Pullen), and Simon of Poissy, of whom John said that he was a *fidus lector sed obtusior disputator*.[3] According to his own reckoning, John put in about twelve years as a student.

After this John seems to have gone to Italy, where he entered papal service. When he returned in 1148 to the Coun-

---

[2] *Polycraticus*, II, 28, Cf. C. C. J. Webb, *John of Salisbury* (London, 1932), p. 3.
[3] Cf. Document 1, Appendix.

cil of Rheims he visited his former masters and was deeply disillusioned to find them still logic-chopping at the same old stand. Retracing his steps to Rome after the Council, he entered the service of Eugene III (1145–1153), and remained briefly in that of his successor, Anastasius IV (1153–1154). In 1154 he came back to Archbishop Theobald's service at Canterbury, which became his base of operations during the next twenty years, although he frequently went on papal missions. In 1159 John noted that he had already crossed the Alps *ten* times. Seven of these twenty years he spent in exile because he would not bow before Henry II and his ideas of royal supremacy in ecclesiastical matters. During this period of his life, when he was somewhat under royal censure, he found time to complete his two principal works, the *Polycraticus* and the *Metalogicon*. Both were dedicated to Thomas Becket.

In his *Metalogicon* John not only pleads for literary studies but strongly defends a humane psychology of education, giving us his own acute analysis of the educational practices and practitioners of his day. He could speak with authority. He had been trained by the best teachers of the time. John defends the *trivium* and *quadrivium* against a group of newcomers in the field of educational theory whom he calls "Cornificians." Their doctrine comes to this: facility in reasoning and argumentation is the result of natural talent and exercise and not the product of the formal training of a school. Before turning his attention to the defense of dialectic, John first established the necessity and advantages of the study of grammar and rhetoric. For this our author was well equipped, and a list of the sources of the *Metalogicon* reads like an "index for a

14

combined abridged edition of the Teubner series and the *Patrologiae ... latina.*"[4]

The educational theory of John of Salisbury was clearly Christian. He remarked, "there are many things which do not admit of disputations and which transcend human reason and are consecrated to faith alone" (*Metalogicon*, III, 10). Our mind attains true knowledge, and this is the beginning of his theory of education; for him truth is the conformity of thought with fact. He preferred the Aristotelian explanation that our concepts do have objective validity and foundation in fact but that there are no universal ideas existing as such. The later theory of the universals "*cum fundamento in re*," and the explanation of the origin of our ideas, were not yet worked out in his day. John did not class himself either as a nominalist or as a conceptualist. In the pursuit of knowledge he argued that a person goes through three stages: first there is "opinion," deriving its data from the senses and imagination; next comes

[4] Among the authors he uses are Plato, Aristotle, Hippocrates, Porphyry, Dionysius the pseudo-Areopagite, Terence, Cicero, Catullus, Julius Caesar, Publius Syrus, Vergil, Horace, Seneca the Elder, Ovid, Valerius Maximus, Lucan, Pliny, Quintilian, Martial, Juvenal, Suetonius, Aulus Gellius, Apuleius, Chalcidius, Marius Victorinus, Donatus, Palladius, Hilary of Poitiers, Plautus, Servius, Vegetius, Ambrose, Jerome, Augustine, Macrobius, Martianus Capella, Sidonius Apollinaris, Boethius, Fulgentius, Priscian, Cassiodorus, Gregory, Isidore of Seville, Bede, Theodulus, Alcuin, John Scotus, Angelomus of Luxeuil, Remigius, Anselm of Canterbury, Bernard of Chartres, Roscelin, Abelard, Hugh of St. Victor, Theodoric (Thierry) of Chartres, Gilbert de la Porrée, William of Conches, Adam du Petit Pont and Tenred of Dover. Among all these Plato and Aristotle both play a large part. Cf. D. D. McGarry, "Educational Theory in the *Metalogicon* of John of Salisbury," *Speculum*, XXIII, No. 4 (1948), 661.

15

"science," which originates in "reason," an immaterial power transcending sense knowledge but productive of a truth still relative to temporal things; finally comes "understanding" or "wisdom," which is the goal of education. Wisdom is not merely a speculative knowledge but one that should flow over into active life.

But the times were against him, and John of Salisbury's lengthy defense of the traditional arts course did not greatly influence the university movement, where the trend was to emphasize dialectics and philosophy. Some of the cathedral schools, and the monastic schools in general, retained their traditional interpretation of the arts course. But John of Salisbury would have been delighted with the amount of formal training demanded by the medieval university arts course, though doubtless he would have wished to have more lecture time devoted to his beloved classical authors.

THE BEGINNINGS OF THE INTELLECTUAL GUILDS: THE UNIVERSITY OF PARIS

The great cathedrals of Europe, so evident to all, are by no means the only bequest of medieval civilization. Of the great contributions coming from the medieval world, the universities rank very high. They were intellectual cathedrals, not buildings but organizations. They are still with us, and still distinctive of European civilization.

The universities came clearly into historic existence in the late twelfth century. Of their beginnings—as in the case of other important institutions, parliaments for example—there are few historical records. There were two great universities, however, which served as models for the others: the University of Bologna and the University of Paris. Of both, our records, though in some instances late, are extensive enough to give us some understanding of their organization.

The educational emphasis during the eleventh and twelfth centuries moved from grammar to dialectic, and the *trivium* and *quadrivium* were gradually made subordinate to dialectic and the other parts of philosophy. This trend is not strikingly clear until the curriculum decrees for the University of Paris in the middle of the thirteenth century. The newer trends in educational theory, current at the time of the rise of the first universities, looked on the arts as a means to arrive at a philosophical culture. Though some knowledge of the arts was considered a prerequisite for a full philosophical culture, the important point to note is that it is philosophy which takes precedence and not grammar or literature.[5]

There were many factors involved in the rise of the universities. The widening of intellectual horizons through the new knowledge which came into European ken with the discovery and exploitation of the full corpus of Aristotelian writings during the late twelfth and the thirteenth centuries, the renaissance in Roman and ecclesiastical law, the writings of the Greek medical tradition—all these gave impetus to the intellectual movements institutionalized in the nascent universities. There was also the closer connection with Moslem culture and civilization, the growth of urban life with its need for more education, and the higher educational level of churchmen in general. Then, too, the rise of the guilds and various forms of medieval corporativism influenced the organizational

[5] Cf. document in Thorndike, *Univ. Records,* pp. 15–17.

development of the universities. But apart from these general environmental influences there were special causes affecting the two cities, Paris and Bologna, which were to make them the homes of the two archetypal universities.

For much of the twelfth century, the schools of Paris were not as important as they later became. True, Paris was a city blessed with schools, but so also was the city of Chartres. During much of the twelfth century the rivalry between the two was so close that it would have been difficult to predict the dominance of the great University of Paris of the thirteenth century, drawing its students from all over Christendom and receiving the encomiums of the popes. Although Chartres was especially noted for classical studies, and although for a certain period in the twelfth century it was also in the forefront in philosophical studies, events occurred in Paris which gradually centered scholarly interest on that city. The events at Paris seem happy coincidences. They could have happened in other cities as well, but they did not. And their importance is such that, gathered all together, they provide a probable explanation of why Paris and not Chartres, for example, became the goal of scholars.

The twelfth-century student was attracted more by a *teacher* than by the name of a school. In the matter of teachers Paris was fortunate. First she had William of Champeaux, and then later his more famous pupil and chief contradictor, Abelard. Some have seen in Abelard the main reason why the schools of Paris became outstanding so quickly. Certainly, Abelard was one of the important reasons, for his lectures drew students by the thousands, and the echoes of his various disputes, especially his frontal attack on his former teacher, William of

Champeaux, resounded throughout the intellectual world of his day. The disputes of Abelard and those of other teachers at Paris made the city a center of the new dialectical theology and a hot-bed of controversy. Every teacher knows that where there is a great deal of discussion there is at least a great deal of interest; and, where one has interest, one has many students. The more the interest grows, the more the student body grows. In those days the presence of a famous master meant a famous school. Abelard and teachers like him created a set of disciples about themselves, stimulated discussions and interest, and were succeeded by a group of scholarly clerics at Paris who forwarded by their talents the impetus given to the new intellectual movements. Thus the University of Paris went forward quickly in its development.

A second important factor was the specialization at Paris in *theological* matters. Such specialization attracted the notice of foreign students and masters, people like Stephen Langton, Nicholas Breakspear, later Pope Adrian IV (1154–1159), or the German Ludolph of Magdebourg. This specialization in the "queen of the sciences" also attracted the notice of the papal chancery, and the University of Paris soon became the favorite of the popes. Pope Innocent III (1198–1216) gave Paris its first official charter, and from subsequent popes came more charters and favors which helped greatly to give the university that theological leadership which it held for so many centuries.

Furthermore, Paris possessed a number of individual schools. There was the cathedral school at which William of Champeaux was presiding when Abelard entered the arena to begin those controversies which formed so great a part of their relationship, as the former pupil developed into a competing and then conquering master. There was another school on the left bank of the Seine, connected with the church of Ste. Geneviève. Here Abelard presided for some time. Finally, there should be noted the group of teachers and scholars at the church of the Canons Regular of St. Victor, which became a school of positive and traditional theology, where some of the chief opponents of the new dialectical methods lectured. The part that men like Hugh of St. Victor played in the development of Scholasticism has frequently been all but forgotten.

These are perhaps the chief "accidental" events that combined to aid Paris in establishing herself as one of the intellectual capitals of Christendom from the thirteenth century onwards. These were the environmental conditions in which the university developed, but to trace the actual steps by which this growth came about, the historical records are lacking. It would almost seem that, like Topsy, the university just grew. Some scholars have seen in the widespread guild movements a natural model for the university. In their opinion scholars, like the merchants and craftsmen, organized in a guild system, and thus the university was but the effect of "corporativism" on the intellectual level. This may well have been so, but the documentary proofs have not as yet been discovered in sufficient quantity to trace such a development. The principle, however, that no one could simply set himself up without due training under some master in the branch of knowledge in which he intended to teach others was an accepted one even in Abelard's time, as he found to his sorrow.

The great historian of organizational development in the medieval universities, Dean Rashdall, has pointed out four stages in the growth of the university at Paris as a corporate organization. The first was the codification of unwritten customs into some sort of a body of written law governing the university. There are clear indications of statutes (although the actual text is not extant) dating from the first years of the thirteenth century. For instance, there is a decree of Pope Innocent III about 1210 dealing with the restitution to the society of masters of a member who had been expelled for a breach of the laws. The statutes referred to in this document concerned the official garment which the professor must wear, the order to be followed in lectures and disputations, and the requirement that masters must attend the funerals of their deceased colleagues. These passing references evidently indicate a body of detailed statutes, but we do not possess their actual text.

A second characteristic is found in the legal right of a corporation to sue or be sued, and there are indications that the university had such rights at this same period; for instance, another document of Innocent III, who was himself a doctor of Paris University, empowered the masters as a society to elect a proctor to represent them at the papal court in Rome, and in 1212 there was a lawsuit between the chancellor (the diocesan authority empowered to grant the license, or permission to teach) and the university. In this case the pope supported the university against the chancellor.

Thirdly, an official seal was needed to affix to the bond to insure repayment when money was borrowed, and the university had to have money to pay its legal representative at Rome. Medieval men loved to have their special seal, much as their modern successors demand official stationery. There is

21

an interesting instance in 1284 of a large body of Pisan citizens captured by Genoa in one of the frequent inter-city wars who were kept in prison for eighteen years, and who used a seal entitled *"Sigillum Universitatis Carceratorum Januae Detentorum"*!

Finally, to go about the business of collecting money and directing legal procedures, the university needed some officials, and this gave further form to its rapidly developing organization.

In the matter of definite dates, we have the first official statutes given by the papal legate, Cardinal Robert de Courçon, in the year 1215.[6] There is a further development in the famous "Magna Carta" of Paris University given in the papal document of Gregory IX (1227–1241). By this instrument the pope authorized the university to make its own laws and rules for courses and studies, gave it a separate papal jurisdiction (no longer merely diocesan), and enlarged the course of studies. With this document the university comes of age and appears in legal history as a fully formed intellectual corporation for the advancement and training of scholars.[7]

THE INTELLECTUAL GUILDS OF BOLOGNA

As Paris was generally given the highest place in the philosophical and theological circles of the medieval world, so Bologna and its "universities" occupied a like position with regard to the study of civil and canon law. It would seem that, as dialectic was singled out from the seven liberal arts for

[6] Cf. Document 2, Appendix.
[7] Cf. document in Thorndike, *Univ. Records*, pp. 35–39.

22

special emphasis at Paris, and this special study and the enthusiasm engendered by its application to theological problems attracted both students and famous masters to Paris, so at Bologna it was grammar, and especially the tradition of rhetoric, among the arts, which formed a traditional basis for the study of law. The tradition of rhetorical and juridical studies had never been completely lost in Italy despite the barbarian invasions and the administrative breakdown of the Roman Empire. The invading barbarians had found themselves not only in a definite minority of numbers with regard to their conquered populations, but also without anything comparable to the body of laws that governed the Roman provincials. As a result the various barbarian codes were drawn up in the Visigothic, Burgundian, and Lombard sections, for example. In northern Italy (Lombardy), where the Lombards had established themselves and gradually begun to take on at least a veneer of Roman civilization, Lombard and Roman laws were both taught to students. The problem is to discover how much of the great codes of Justinian were actually known in the time between the death of Gregory I (604) and the end of the eleventh century, and so far it would seem that there is no indication of any use of the *Digest* during these centuries. On the other hand, there was a tradition of legal teaching, and notaries and judges were trained in the Italian schools. Lanfranc, when he came to England, brought with him a traditional knowledge and practice of law which played an important part in the formation of the English ecclesiastical law.

This legal tradition, and later the great renaissance in Roman law which marked the rise of the University of Bologna, were of great importance in gaining for that university a leadership

23

in legal studies which it held for many centuries. Of the other centers of legal studies before Bologna's rise to headship, probably Pavia and Ravenna are the most important. Pavia was especially important for Lombard law, while at Ravenna imperial traditions had kept alive the learning of earlier centuries, and connections with the later Holy Roman Empire had aided in their preservation and renewed application. But Bologna had an excellent geographical position as a meeting place of the roads from Rome, Ravenna, Pisa, and Pavia, and this may possibly be another factor to explain its rise as a university center.

In addition there were probably several schools in Bologna. There was a type of municipal school common to the Italian cities, where rhetoric was stressed, an episcopal school (although not all scholars admit this school at Bologna), and a monastic school. It is said that the University of Bologna owes its existence to all three of these elements—the episcopal school contributing the foundation studies in arts, the municipal school the study of Roman civil law, and the monastic school, especially that of St. Felix, the study of canon law.

Bologna, too, had her famous men, who arrived at just the right moment. During the first half of the twelfth century came Irnerius, the renovator of Roman law, and one of the founders of the University of Bologna. He was famous by 1116 and, though he died before 1140, his achievements were far-reaching. He introduced the study of the whole of Roman law through the Justinian codes, and he provided a method of "glossing," or adding explanations to the text with notes, parallel passages, and variants. Irnerius also developed a kind

24

of legal casuistry as well as the practice of condensing certain texts into maxims which could serve as principles. By such means he brought out clearly certain legal problems. He and his successors at Bologna used their methods on a great part of the *Digest* and *Institutes* of Justinian's codes, and thus the tradition of great schools of law was built up at Bologna, a tradition which lasted throughout the Middle Ages and into modern times. The phrase *"Bononia docet"* became synonymous with the best legal training to be had, and just as the theology which was developed in the University of Paris became the theology of Europe, so too the civil and canonical jurisprudence of Bologna became European.

Bologna was not only fortunate in finding a great teacher of the civil law and a renovator of the Justinian codes, but by a remarkable coincidence the greatest name in canon law, the law of the Church, was also a teacher there. A monk working quietly—in fact so quietly that scholars have great difficulty in assigning an exact date to his work—Gratian of the monastery of St. Felix produced about the year 1140 a codification of canon law which deeply influenced European civilization. Before his time the mass of Church law had been composed of large collections, incompletely and poorly arranged and abounding in contradictions. From this mass of materials—i.e., laws of Church councils and local synods, decrees, letters of the popes—Gratian produced his *Decretum,* a work containing about 3,900 laws, or "canons."

But Gratian's work was not merely one of collection. He not only collected and compiled but used a systematic approach which grouped the authorities in a methodical way

25

and drew from the accumulated texts exact notions about the nature of law and its origins. He was able to profit from the work done by Abelard, and the methods of *Sic et Non* are to be found here—for instance, the lining up of different opinions and the fundamental notions of the various meanings that can be given to the same word in different authorities and texts. Peter Lombard, in writing his *Sentences* (about 1150), was in his turn able to use the work of Gratian; and so the methods pioneered and popularized by the inveterate disputant, Abelard, became fundamental to the two great branches of ecclesiastical science through the *Decretum* of Gratian for canon law and through the *Sentences* of Peter Lombard for theology. Abelard had built better than he knew.

Medieval people no less than modern ones loved to have definite knowledge about the beginnings of things. Whenever they were dealing with an institution that went "beyond the memory of man," they gave it considerable antiquity. So it is not surprising that by the thirteenth century there was a legend to the effect that Bologna had been founded by Theodosius II in the year 433. In defense of this legend a charter was produced; indeed the defenders overshot the mark a bit, for they produced *two* charters!

Historical record has a much more modest account to render. The first recorded legal recognition that we have is a decree (ancient enough in university history) of Frederick I (1152–1190), called the *Habita* and issued in 1158. The decree is a charter granting to students a special ecclesiastical jurisdiction. Some think it was meant to be restricted to Bologna, others interpret it as "a general privilege conferred on the student class throughout the Lombard Kingdom." At any rate, it is a *de facto* recognition of the existence of a school of law at Bologna. Another confirmation comes in a document of 1189, a papal document of Clement III (1187–1191) which confirmed an already existing legatine ordinance forbidding masters or scholars to offer to the landlord a higher rent for a house than the one paid by scholars already living there. This is certainly a legal detail indicating that things must have been rather well-organized on the Bologna University campus long before this time.

It is clear, then, that a university was developing at Bologna contemporaneously with that of Paris, and by the thirteenth century each city had one of the new intellectual guilds well on the way to permanent organization. It is true, as will be seen, that the University of Bologna is, strictly speaking, two "universities," and that the university organization at Bologna was somewhat different from that at Paris. Basically, however, at both places there was the same idea of assembling skilled scholars to train unskilled apprentices in knowledge, and the actual functions of both groups are remarkably similar.

Both Paris and Bologna were models which other university groups copied in their own organization during the thirteenth, fourteenth, and fifteenth centuries. It will be helpful then, in order to gain a fairly adequate knowledge of the ground lines of university work and functions, to study these two great archetypes, noting their administrational organization, their curricula and academic grades, the problems they faced in their environment, and the influence which they exerted upon the medieval world.

27

ADDITIONAL READINGS*

Abelson, P., *Seven Liberal Arts, a Study in Medieval Culture* (New York, 1906).

Adamson, J. W., "Education," *The Legacy of the Middle Ages*, edited by C. G. Crump and E. F. Jacob (Oxford, 1927).

Brown, M .A., "John of Salisbury," *Franciscan Studies*, XIX (1959), 240–297.

Compayre, G., *Abelard and the Origin and Early History of Universities* (New York, 1893).

Deanesley, M., "Early Medieval Schools," *Cambridge Medieval History*, V.

Haarhoff, T. J., *Schools of Gaul* (1920, Reprint, 1958).

Haskins, C. H., *The Renaissance of the Twelfth Century* (Cambridge, 1927).

——, *The Rise of the Universities* (New York, 1923), Paperback, Chapter I.

Hunt, R., "English Learning in the Late 13th Century," *Transactions of the Royal Historical Society*, XIX (1936).

Kuttner, Stephen, "The Father of the Science of Canon Law," *Jurist*, I (1941), 2–19.

McGarry, Daniel, "Educational Theories of John of Salisbury," *Speculum*, XXIII (1948), 659–675.

——, trans., *The Metalogicon of John of Salisbury* (Berkeley, Calif., 1955).

McMahon, Clara P., *Education in Fifteenth-Century England*, The Johns Hopkins University Studies, No. 35 (Baltimore, 1947), Chapters I–III.

Mullinger, J., *The Schools of Charles the Great* (London, 1877).

* The additional readings are intended for undergraduates and have been restricted usually to brief selections in English. Lengthier treatment and additional bibliographical data are to be found in A. Sorbelli, *Storia della Universita di Bologna*, I (Bologna, 1944), and Stephen d'Irsay, *Histoire des Universités*, I (Paris, 1933), and of course the Powicke-Emden edition of Rashdall's *Universities* mentioned in this list. But the volume of P. Kibre, *The Nations in the Mediaeval Universities* (Mediaeval Academy of America, 1958) has more recent bibliographical references.

Rand, E. K., "Classics in the Thirteenth Century," *Speculum,* IV (1929), 249–269.

Rashdall, H., Powicke, F. M., Emden, A. B., *The Universities of Europe in the Middle Ages* (Oxford, 1936), 3 vols. The various sections in the first and third volumes referring to topics mentioned in the first section of this essay give much additional information and copious notes. The index is in the third volume, and constant reference to it is necessary to use the volumes efficiently.

Singer, C., "School of Salerno," *History,* X (1925), 242–246.

Thorndike, L., "Elementary and Secondary Education in the Middle Ages," *Speculum,* XV (1940), 400–408.

Vaughan, E. V., *Origins and Early Development of the English Universities to the Close of the 13th Century,* University of Missouri Studies, Social Science Series, II, No. 1 (1908).

Williams, John R., "The Cathedral School of Rheims in the 11th Century," *Speculum,* XXIX (1954), 661–677.

II. CONSTITUTIONAL DEMOCRACY
AT THE UNIVERSITY LEVEL:
THE NATIONS

One of the most interesting developments in the medieval universities is that of the *nations*. This "campus" organization developed both at Bologna and Paris, but with considerable differences. At Bologna the nations are organizations of students; at Paris they are societies of masters. Although the earliest statutes known to us come from Paris, there are indications that nations were formed at Bologna even earlier. Du Boulay's description of a Parisian nation is that of "a corporation or association of masters, teaching . . . all the arts and inscribed in the same roll and living under the same law and ordinances."[1] But at Bologna the nation can best be pictured as a subdivision within the "university" of out-of-town students who have banded together for mutual protection, help, and collective security against local authorities. Perhaps the term "nation" may have been used to designate a foreign student. At any rate, in the fourteenth-century Bologna regulations, where the student was born determined the nation to which he was assigned.

[1] Quoted by P. Kibre, *The Nations in the Mediaeval Universities* (Cambridge, 1948), p. 3.

30

THE NATIONS AT BOLOGNA

In 1158 Emperor Frederick I issued a decree, *Authentica Habita*, giving scholars the right to be tried by either their own masters or the bishop rather than by the city magistrates. Freed from local jurisdiction, the foreign students seemed to have formed *collegia*, or nations, for the purpose of mutual benefits and fraternity. These smaller groups, or guilds, then coalesced to form "two universities," the *universitas ultramontanorum* for those coming from beyond the mountains or outside Italy, and the *universitas citramontanorum* for students from the Italian peninsula and nearby islands. Neither of these universities included students from the city of Bologna itself. Originally, the student universities were interested in matters relating to mutual protection and left academic concerns to the professors. For the most part citizens of Bologna, the professors formed *collegia*, or guilds, of their own. As the power of the universities grew, these succeeded in gaining control over academic affairs in general.

The commune of Bologna long struggled to prevent the growth of the student universities, claiming that these students "did not make a class by themselves but were only pupils of the doctors of the law." But the students found a protector in Pope Honorius III (1216–1227). He intervened in their behalf in 1217 and urged them not to dissolve their societies as the commune demanded. Later on, he protected them against Frederick II (1211–1250), who attempted to close the *studium* at Bologna by an edict (1225) ordering both students and professors to set out for Naples and his own newly founded university there. The edict was generally disregarded and at

31

papal insistence was later repealed. When the city fathers at Bologna realized that they could not prevent the formation of these strong student guilds and saw the economic and prestige benefits of a university, they reversed their field and tried to attract students to their city by means of exemptions from military service, city taxes, and tolls on their books. In 1245 the students were finally given the same legal rights as citizens, excepting political rights. Sometimes students who had lived at Bologna for more than ten years were granted actual citizenship, but then they lost their university rights and privileges.

Both of the jurist universities were subdivided into smaller groups, the nations. In 1265 the fourteen nations of the ultramontane university were reduced to thirteen; about one hundred and seventy years later (1432), their number was sixteen. In 1265, the fourteen nations of the ultramontane university included the French, Spanish, Provençal, English, Picard, Burgundian, Poitevin, Tourainian, Norman, Catalonian, Hungarian, Polish, German and Gascon. Though the cisalpine university in the thirteenth and fourteenth centuries seems to have had but four main divisions, composed of students from Rome, Campania, Tuscany, and Lombardy, by 1400 it had three nations, Lombard, Tuscan, and Roman, with further subdivisions in each of them; for example, in 1432, the Tuscan nation was subdivided into Florence, Pisa (including Lucca), Siena, Spoleto, Ravenna, and Venice. Each of these various subdivisions had one *consilarius*, or representative, in the university congregation, with one vote, except those of Rome and Sicily, each of which had two representatives and two votes. Later on, the Tuscan nation acquired another subdivision for students from Sardinia and Cyprus, with one vote, finally bringing the total votes of the cisalpine university up to seventeen, equal to the ultramontane, which had also developed seventeen.

Besides the two jurist universities, another university came into existence at Bologna during the second half of the thirteenth century. It was composed of students in arts and medicine. This university was made up of four nations, the Ultramontane, Lombard, Tuscan and Roman. At first it had no separate rector, but was under the two jurist universities. In 1268 the newcomer had secured permission to elect its own rector, but the commune of Bologna cancelled this privilege in 1295. The students, however, patiently continued to elect their own rector, and at last a compromise was worked out in 1316 between the two law universities and the city magistrates which gave equal recognition to all three universities. The rector of the third university was to be elected in turn from each of that university's four nations, and each nation had two representatives in the university congregation, except the Lombard nation, which had three. Elected every three months, these representatives were to aid and advise the rector, whom, according to the constitutions, they could remove if need be.

The nations at Bologna had certain features which distinguished them from the similarly named organizations at the University of Paris. First of all, they were composed of non-Bolognese students only, originating probably as voluntary organizations of students from the same districts, who would naturally tend to join together. Students who were citizens of Bologna were not allowed in the nations, nor were members of the nations regarded as citizens of the commune. Throughout the long history of the university, the city magistrates gave many privileges to the foreign students, but citizenship was seldom granted. Secondly, the nations and the universities at Bologna were at first confined to students of law. It was only in the second half of the thirteenth century that a university for students of arts and medicine was allowed to form, and even then several decades passed before this new university was able to secure equality with the two older law universities.

The formation of these universities had been unsuccessfully opposed by both the professors and the commune. The professors were excluded from the nations; and the commune, not unnaturally, probably feared the possible abuse of power by irresponsible student rectors. By repeated threatened or actual migrations, however, and more especially through the constant defense and help of the various popes, the student universities gradually won out. By the second half of the thirteenth century they were sharing, through their nations and elected representatives, not only in the election of their own rector but also in the general administration and direction of the *studium generale* itself.

Organization and Activities of the Nations at Bologna

In trying to picture the actual functioning of the nations at Bologna, the scarcity of source material is a chief difficulty. Our earliest collection of statutes dates from 1317–1347, and these statutes were made jointly by both the jurist universities. In regard to the individual nations, there is a collection of records of the German nation, but it is dated 1497. Fortunately, although the collection bears so late a date, there are earlier statutes mentioned in it, and the general conservativeness of the medieval university tends to increase our confidence that it can be safely used to describe the nation during the late thirteenth and the whole fourteenth century. The German nation, however, had a somewhat special organization and held a more honorable position in the ultramontane university than the others, evidenced by its two votes in the election of the rector and in the university assemblies. Moreover, the rector once every five years, had to be selected from the German nation.

The German nation had two chief officials called *proctors*; the other nations but one. These proctors had jurisdiction over the members of the German nation, who were thus partly removed from the jurisdiction both of the rector and the city magistrates. Furthermore, the students of the German nation who were of the nobility were not subject to the obedience of the rector. The proctors' duties were carefully outlined in the nation's statutes and a record was kept of their fulfillment. The first of their duties was a perennial one—they had to collect the dues. These dues, varying in accordance with the income of the student, were paid upon entrance into the nation. Some students might give additional money, and there were "special assessments" as well as voluntary gifts and bequests from former students to aid in keeping the books balanced. Gifts might come from a member who felt he had been remiss in his duty, or from some newly made master or doctor. Another kind of revenue came from the fines which the nation collected. But in spite of all these varied revenues, the books would not always balance, and we read of the nation's belongings finding their way to a local pawnbroker to obtain suddenly needed cash.

The proctors were on a tight budget, owing to various kinds of expenditures. The special religious services of the nation necessitated payments to be made to officiating clergy and to singers; additional sums were needed for candles, Mass wine, and the general upkeep of the nation's own chapel. In 1317 the German nation spent forty *solidi* for long benches for the church, and in 1346 money was needed to repair the choir stalls. There were also expenditures for "conviviality." Banquets and celebrations became more lavish as time went on, and the costs for wines, spices, cakes, and suchlike put a heavy burden on the treasury. In addition to the usual holy days of the Church, the German nation had a special devotion to St. Catherine, St. Nicholas, and St. Martin; from 1292 on they had a special Mass said each Sunday in honor of Our Lady. Then, too, there were wages to pay to the nation's beadle, contributions to the salaries of the university beadle and notary, and fees to the lawyers who handled the nation's frequent legal quarrels and to the nation's doctor. At other times there might be extraordinary expenses, such as occurred in 1321, when the nation paid the expenses of their proctors summoned by the rectors to Imola during the suspension of the *studium* in that year.

Besides collecting the revenues of the nation, the proctors kept the inventory of the possessions of the nation, the matriculation rolls, the statute books, and the books recording the privileges of the nation. When their term of office was up, they turned in the inventory of the possessions and the accounts of the money collected and disbursed. If members were sick or dying, it was the proctor's duty to visit and console them. If the sick man was in material need, the proctor provided him with food and money out of special collections or from the general funds. When a member died, the proctor arranged for the funeral.

The proctors kept a wary eye on student debts and saw to it that no student left the university until he had satisfied his creditors. If the student departed without doing so, he was deprived of membership in the nation until he had paid his debts, and notices to this effect would be sent to him or his relatives. In 1322, several students left Bologna without paying their debts to a certain man, Blenkymus by name, who quickly made his woes known to the authorities. Notice was sent to the bishop of Strasbourg, under whose jurisdiction they were, that because of their failure to pay their debts these men were suspended from the nation's membership both at Bologna and Padua and would remain suspended until they had paid said Blenkymus.

Another fruitful source of problems for proctors came from students' quarrels. It was the duty of the proctor to try to persuade the contending parties to compose their differences and to omit nothing which might bring them back to peace and unity. If he failed and the disputants refused his terms, then each party selected a student from the nation and the proctor picked a third. These three judges rendered a decision within a month of the date of their selection, and if one party refused to accept the decision agreed to by the other two, that person or group was subject to a fine. No member could call in an outsider to act as judge, and the dispute must be reported to the proctors. If a member violated this rule, he was subject to fine.

As administrative heads of the nation, the proctors convoked and presided over the meetings of the nation. These meetings were usually held in the nation's own church or chapel, which for the German nation was that of St. Frediano. If the city gates were closed, because of war or riots, the meetings were held inside the walls at some other church. Attendance was compulsory and absence punishable by fine. If the rector at the time happened to be chosen from the German nation, he did not have to come unless the proctor thought it necessary.

The proctors were chosen annually on the feast of the Epiphany (January 6), with each of the retiring proctors selecting a candidate from among those present. The members then voted, and the candidate obtaining a majority vote was considered elected. In the second half of the fourteenth century, the German nation seems to have changed to a system of electors with one for each of the four important German principalities of Swabia, Bavaria, Franconia, and Saxony, who, together with the two retiring proctors, elected the new proctors by written ballot. Later on, they returned to the first method of election. The candidate for the office of proctor had to be at least twenty years of age, and must not have made any pre-election promises or engaged in any political manipulations; either, if discovered, would disqualify him. Immediately upon election, the new proctors formally accepted and took the oath of office before the assembly. If they refused to accept the election results and their office as proctor, they would be expelled from the nation. Their first official act was to appoint two "syndics" who were to help them in the performance of their office. Each proctor had to promise that he would turn over, on expiration of his term of office, the books and funds of the nation.

The nation also owned its own treasure chest, which was kept in a special place—in the case of the German nation, in the church of St. Frediano. It was locked with two separate keys, each of the proctors having but one. In this box were kept the nation's seal, vestments, and Mass books. Sometimes, because of the suspension of the *studium*, plagues, or wars, the treasure chest had to be stored. The German nation selected the convent of the Dominicans or Franciscans, as is noted in their records together with the amounts that had to be paid for transportation of the box.

From the records of the nation and its functions, it is clear that it resembled a religious guild more than an academic organization. Thus in the records of the German nation there is no mention of academic matters, except for the custom that the proctor must accompany a member of the nation who is about to receive the licentiate or doctorate in canon or civil law. The nations shared in the academic life of the university through their elected representatives in the university assemblies, where the business of actually running the *studium* was conducted.

The Consilarii

Unfortunately not much recorded information about the other nations at the universities of Bologna has survived. The indications are that the heads of these nations were given the name of *consilarii*, and they seem to have been advisors to the rector rather than the executive heads of their nations. These *consilarii* were subject to the rector, while the two proctors of the German nation were subject to the nation rather than to the rector. For this reason, seemingly, it was not permissible to hold the office of the rector and proctor of the German nation simultaneously. The position of *consilarius* was next in importance to that of the rector, but precisely what his duties were with regard to his own nation we are not certain. One of his known duties was to report within ten days, both to the rector and the treasurer of the university, all the names of new students who had entered his nation. If he failed in this, he would be fined heavily. He presented the graduates from his own nation to the rector and arranged for their public and private examinations. But his most important duties were in connection with his membership in the university senate. As the rector's advisor, he was to come whenever summoned by him to give advice and counsel and must promise to keep secret the proceedings of the meetings. The beadle of the university summoned these *consilarii*, or proctors, and a two-thirds attendance of their number would constitute a quorum.

In elections the matter was decided by a majority vote, and the voting might be done either by a ballot or by means of the "black-and-white-bean" vote. In this second method, a white bean signified the affirmative and a black, the negative. Each member was given two beans, one black and one white. Only one proposition could be voted on at a time. While passing the box, the beadle or notary was not to look as the bean was dropped in; but if it appeared that someone had dropped in both the beans, the collector could throw the contents of the box on the floor and the guilty party would lose his vote. If the notary or beadle was considered to be more than ordinarily interested in the elections, two friars were given charge of the collection of the votes. The actual counting was done with the rector looking over the teller's shoulders. Evidently discussions reached more than academic warmth at times, for there was a regulation that members of the assembly might not come armed. If someone felt the need of carrying his weapon, he was excused from the convocation. The *consilarius* in nations other than the German was usually appointed by the retiring *consilarius*, but sometimes he was elected by the nation at large, with a plurality of votes. He could not stand for re-election for the succeeding term. The *consilarius* took an oath of obedience to the rector, since he was himself a university student.

The Rector

One of the most important duties of the *consilarius* as a member of the university senate was the election of the rector.[2] Qualifications for the rector were the following: he must be near his twenty-fifth year, have studied law for five years, be unmarried, a cleric, a student from the university from which he was chosen, possessed of discretion, prudence, honesty, gravity, and talents that would make him useful to the whole university. During his term of office he was not to go about armed unless the need was so clear that the majority of the university members had given their approval. The rector of the ultramontane university was chosen on the first of May, and an election dispute in 1256 had brought about a fixed system of rotating the office so that the rector was selected from one group of nations one year and another group the next, on a four-year cycle. The voters were the nations, each nation having one vote except the German nation, which had

[2] Cf. document in Thorndike, *Univ. Records*, pp. 163–166.

two. The cismontane rector was elected by the nineteen *consilarii*, six each from the Roman and Tuscan and seven from the Lombard nation, in addition to nineteen other voters selected from their respective nations in the same proportion. The cismontane rector was also elected on the first of May, and choice of the candidate for this office followed a three-year cycle; each year the choice was made from a different nation. The electors voted by ballot, but absentee ballots were forbidden.

Election day saw great feasting, much of it at the expense of the new rector. Usually the rector was from a prominent family, since he needed to be fairly wealthy to support his rank. Because the university contained a large number of clerics, and since canon law forbade a layman to have jurisdiction over clerics, the rector had to be a cleric. Generally he was a beneficed ecclesiastic, dean, or canon. Although expensive, the office of rector had its honors. The incumbent took precedence in processions over all other dignitaries including cardinals, with the exception of the bishop of Bologna. He was also given an honorarium of one hundred Bolognese pounds (but this last is in a statute dated 1474).

As chief magistrate of the university, the rector claimed civil and criminal jurisdiction over both students and professors, although this authority was only partly recognized. His criminal jurisdiction was limited to minor matters after 1544. The rectors judged disputes between the law universities. If there was a public argument between professor and students, the rector acted as arbiter. An appeal might be taken from him to the university and from the university to the papal legate.

As an administrative official, the rector derived his authority from the statutes which had been enacted by the whole university and which he himself took an oath to observe and enforce. He also promised that he would see to an honest election of his successor. Moreover, he was bound to stay in town one month after the end of his term in case anything should be found awry in his administration or books. Should he have to depart before the month had elapsed, he must deposit a bond in his absence. As noted above, the students, with the exception of the German students, had to take an oath of obedience to both rector and statutes. If they disobeyed the laws, the rector could impose penalties or fines. For more serious crimes the rector pronounced sentence of suspension from the university rights and privileges; if the crime was unusually serious, he could extend exclusion to descendants of the culprit, provided a majority of his proctors concurred. In his relations with the city fathers, the rector had supervision over rents and repairs in houses rented or owned by students, as well as control over tradesmen and those engaged in the copying and publication of books. His sanctions against offenders in these matters were the interdict, fines, or boycotts. To enforce civil penalties, the rector had to rely on co-operation from the head official of the commune, the *podestà*. Should it happen that the town official refused redress when a student was injured, the rector, with a two-thirds approval of his advisors, could invoke that most forceful of medieval university weapons, the suspension of lectures, or the "university strike." This meant the temporary closing of the university and might even lead to its removal to a more hospitable city.

The rector exercised supervision over the various types of

scribes who corrected, copied, illuminated, or bound the manuscript, or handwritten, textbooks. It was up to him to see that bells were rung on time and that the salaries of the doctors were paid. Each one of the two rectors of the jurist universities held one of the three keys necessary to open the treasure chest, or *archa*, of the university, and the third key was held for six months by a member of the cismontane, and the next six months by a member of the ultramontane, university. Whoever held the third key had to be approved by a majority of both universities. The rector also presided over the examinations and at graduation ceremonies. It is interesting to note that the rector had a secret commission of four students, two from each of the universities, who had to report within a period of three days any doctor who did not finish his assigned material, did not start on time, or did not make use of the disputation method. The lectures of the professor were regulated by the statutes of the university.

Other University Officials

To aid them in conducting the *studium*, the rector and his advisors elected four *syndics*, two from each university. The syndics watched their respective rectors to prevent fraud and to audit the accounts. There was also a group of six "prudent" clerics, three from each university, who acted as judges and examiners when scribes were accused of editing incorrect or corrupt texts. The people most closely watched in this matter were the *stationarii*, or bookstore people, who both sold books and had them copied. At stated times they submitted the master text to the members of this supervising board. If they were using a poor text for their copies, they were fined; half of the fine went to the one discovering the error—which undoubtedly evoked more than ordinary examining interest in the board members. Copies of textbooks of both professors and students were also examined by this group, whose members were called *peciarii* after the word *pecia*, a section of the approved original of a handwritten textbook.[3]

The rector and his advisors also selected the *massarii*, who performed the duties of treasurers. Each university nominated and voted separately on its candidates before the names were submitted to the vote of the other university. Those elected took an oath to perform their job honestly and put up a bond of one hundred Bolognese pounds.

The officials who did most of the odd jobs were the university beadles. There was a general beadle who was the public address system of the university, announcing disputations, lectures, feast days, and books for sale. He accompanied the rector on all public occasions, such as funerals or processions, and on his visits to the commune *podestà*. For his remuneration the beadle was dependent on the generosity of the students. He was allowed to take up two collections, one before Christmas, the other before Easter. Then there were other "special" beadles whose duties were much like those of school janitors; in the winter, they kept a sufficient supply of straw on the floor, not to sit on but to keep the students' feet warm; in the summertime, they had to clean their schoolrooms twice a month. These beadles saw to it that the roof did not leak and

[3] Cf. document in Thorndike, *Univ. Records*, pp. 166–168.

that windows were covered, for books left in the school were their responsibility. Beadles were to be present when treatises were begun and at the *repetitiones*, which were lectures in which portions of class matter or related topics were treated in greater detail. None of the officials elected by the rector and his advisors could be removed without the consent of the university in a general assembly. In case the incumbent should die or resign, there were elaborate rules for the selection of the new office-holder.

General Convocations

At the general convocation thirty-eight students, nineteen from each university, were selected, in manner and number as was done for the *consilarii*. These students in turn elected by ballot the doctors to the four salaried chairs in canon and civil law. At least by 1291, these salaries were paid by the commune, which also paid for the salaried chairs in the university of arts and medicine, so that the professors would not be tempted to seek better positions elsewhere. At this assembly, the texts to be used, the method to be followed by doctors in their lectures, and the amount of material to be covered were decided upon, although the actual prescriptions of these decisions had been already drawn up by a committee of six, selected by a majority vote of the rector and his advisors. The assembly also agreed upon the topics for disputation and the rules governing the actual disputations. Questions of interpretation of the university statutes were settled by a committee of the rectors and three doctors, two in canon and one in civil law. The decision accepted by three of the committee would be valid, but only for the particular case. Once every ten years several revisions of the statutes were made by a committee of eight selected by the rectors and their advisors.

The assembly of the university of arts and medicine apportioned the number of medical students in anatomy who could attend the dissections of human cadavers. Usually some twenty or thirty students, a certain proportion from each nation, were allowed to attend these semi-annual anatomies; a statute of 1442 declared that the commune was to furnish the two cadavers, one male and one female.

From the foregoing description it is evident that not only were the student universities interested in the common welfare of their members, but by the fourteenth century they exerted a real control over the intellectual life of the *studium*. In the fifteenth century—by 1432—the nations as completely independent units seem to have ceased to exist, and some years earlier, in 1405, the office of prior or proctor in several of the ultramontane nations had been suppressed because of frequent discord between the proctor and the rector. But the university itself continued to grow in importance. After 1317 the two law universities acted practically as a unit, using a common law code and common assemblies. If the rector of one university was absent, the other acted for him. The control of the university over the *studium* continued through the sixteenth century; but, by the beginning of the seventeenth century, the commune had taken over most of the privileges once enjoyed by the university. When Napoleon captured Bologna in June, 1796, the nations and their officers were definitely dispersed. In 1798, for the first time in probably more than six hundred years of continued existence, the university of Bologna had a rector who was not a student but a professor.

THE NATIONS AT PARIS

Their Origins

Although adequate source materials are lacking both for the origins of the University of Paris and for the Parisian nations, there is no doubt that in the late twelfth and early thirteenth century scholars from all parts of Europe streamed into Paris, "the source of all knowledge and the well of divine scriptures," according to one medieval enthusiast. With the immigration of so many students from various parts of Europe to Paris, it was only natural that they should band together into groups speaking a common language or from the same district. In the town-and-gown squabbles of 1200, chronicler Roger of Hoveden described how a large group of German clerics were attacked by the provost of the town and his followers. The first documentary mention of the nations seems to be from the year 1222, and from this some have concluded that between the years 1215 and 1222 the nations reached full development. In 1249, there is a document in which the distribution into four nations is made quite clear, but there is no indication as to how long they have been in existence before this date. In 1255, during the quarrels between the mendicant friars and the secular clerics at the university, a letter to Pope Alexander IV (1254–1261) stressed the antiquity of the nations. Since this point strengthened the case of the writers of the letter, their emphasis may have been somewhat exaggerated. At any rate, by the second half of the thirteenth century the nations at Paris had reached full organizational development.

There were only *four* nations at Paris, and their membership

48

was made up of *masters of arts* and not of students in arts. Furthermore, the nations were confined to the faculty of arts alone; there were no nations in medicine, law, or theology. Unlike Bologna, members not only from foreign lands but also from Paris itself were included in them. Many of the masters of arts were students in one of the other faculties because the arts usually formed the prerequisite for entrance into the other faculties. A master of arts, working as a bachelor in medicine, for example, was still a member of his nation and kept this status until he became a doctor. Even after receiving his doctorate in one of the other faculties, he was supposed to remain loyal to his nation according to the oath which he took when he entered the nation, promising that he would "observe and defend the statutes, privileges, liberties and praiseworthy customs . . . of the faculty of arts and of their nation no matter what his station might be."

Why the nations were limited to four is not clear, for the geographical localities of each ranged widely in extent. The French nation included masters from Paris and the surrounding region, from Southern France, Spain, Italy, Greece, and the East. In the fourteenth century, the list of applicants from the French nation for vacant benefices was divided according to the five ecclesiastical provinces of France: Rheims, Sens, Paris, Tours, and Bourges. And Bourges included Spaniards, Italians, Portuguese, and students from Eastern Europe and Asia Minor. The Norman nation enrolled from the Low Countries and from Northern France, and the English nation, the masters from the British Isles, Holland, the Germanies, Sweden, Denmark, Norway, and the Hungarian and Slavic lands. No other nation had so diverse a group of students as

49

the English nation, but it seems that from its beginning the nation was divided into the English and the non-English groups. In the fifteenth century the English nation included three sections: High German, Low German, and Scots. There had been a movement to change the name from the English to the German nation, because there were so few English masters in the nation. This was probably due to the Hundred Years' War (1337–1453), which made it difficult and dangerous for English students to come to Paris.

During the thirteenth and fourteenth centuries, the four nations secured a large amount of independence within the university. Besides its elected officers, each possessed its own schools, chapels, places of assembly, and its own sources of revenues, as well as a special seal, that hallmark of the medieval corporative spirit. This independence of the nation resulted in a strong development of partisan spirit. A student-master was more loyal to his nation than to the university. The nations often quarreled bitterly, not only wasting study time but reducing the university campus to something like a battle-ground. A chief cause was the question of boundary limits. Each nation wished to have a larger number of student-masters on its rolls (*rotuli*) than the others because of the increased prestige deriving from greater numbers, and because more masters meant more initiation fees and a larger treasury.

One unfortunate master expressed a desire to join the French nation, but he happened to be a resident of the Beauvais diocese, which was in Picard territory. The Picards not only claimed but captured him. In the disputes which then ensued other matters were introduced and neither side would come to terms. The French nation withdrew from the union and elected its own rector. An appeal was even made to the king of France, but neither side would accept his decision! Finally, Simon de Brie, the papal legate, successfully settled the quarrel in August, 1266. According to the agreement, which reads like a treaty, both sides had to act in union, all were assured that the degrees granted during the dispute were valid, the double rector system was denounced, and the nations were exhorted to get rid of both incumbents and elect one new rector for all.

Although the legate refused to allow the nations to keep their revenues separately, they did so anyway. The French nation was especially anxious to keep its dues separate because it had many more candidates than the other nations. Concerning the original cause of the quarrels, the legate decreed that in case a scholar was claimed by two nations, the decision should rest with the scholar himself. Twelve years later, in another dispute between the English and Picard nation, the English masters destroyed the houses of the Picards, killed some of the occupants, and drove the others from the city. It was only at the king's intervention that peace was at last secured.

Officials of the Nations

In the earliest records of the nations at Paris the words "proctor" and "rector" were used indiscriminately to describe the head of the nation. Apparently, at that time no chief official for the whole university existed. In 1219 proctors are mentioned as officials in the faculty of arts in charge of collections taken up to pay the travel expenses of the messengers sent by the university to the Holy See at Rome. In 1231, and again in 1237, Pope Gregory IX issued documents forbidding anyone to promulgate a sentence of excommunication against the masters or scholars of the university, their rector or proctor, without permission from Rome. In a document of 1245 the proctors are distinguished from the rector; in 1249 the four proctors to the four nations are named as electors of the rector.

The methods of election of the proctors at Paris were not as well defined as those at Bologna, perhaps because the Bolognese were all apprentice lawyers. Each nation at Paris worked out its own system. In general, the nations agreed that their proctors had to be at least twenty-one years of age and "regent masters"—that is, they had to be teaching in the university when elected. The term of office of the proctors at Paris was only a month (except during the summer vacations), instead of the yearly term at Bologna. In the fifteenth century the proctor of the English nation was still elected every month, but the French nation in 1459 decided that their proctor would serve for two months.

For the election of proctors, electors were chosen according to the nation's local subdivisions. The English nation, however, could not use this type of division because of dissensions, and the majority candidate was chosen regardless of his province within the nation. When the entrants had been all assembled, they usually voted according to the method called "the way of the Holy Spirit." It was so named because, before voting, the electors sang the Latin hymn in honor of the Holy Ghost, *Veni Creator Spiritus*, and then had to make their final decision before a lighted candle (of specified weight, size, and type) had burned out. Another method of election was the *via scrutini*, in which the lector gave his vote in secret to a voting official in order to guard more carefully against fraud or force. The Norman nation had a method peculiar to itself, prized for its antiquity. The system was called "the finding of the black bean" and worked thus. In a hood (examined beforehand to be sure that it was an ordinary one without secret pockets) the beadle placed a quantity of white beans equal to the number of regent masters present, plus a single black bean. The cap or hood was then passed to each of the masters, and whoever drew the black bean named five electors, who then went aside and chose the proctor by a majority vote. This majority candidate, however, had to receive the approval even of the dissenting voters. Despite all these careful prescriptions, the frequent elections were a source of complaint and contention, and the records, which have been preserved, mention accusations of corruption and party politics in the elections of these short-term offices.

At first the proctor collected the dues, and he seems to have been the treasurer. Later on, that duty was given to another official at Paris who was called the *receptor*, or receiver, of the various dues and fines. The proctor became head of the nation at Paris and was a much stronger official than the *consilarius* at Bologna. At installation he received the nation's statutes and seal, and on him devolved the onerous duty of enforcing the rules and regulations of the nation and university. Although he was the connecting link between the nation and the university, his obligation was primarily to his nation. He was bound by oath to punish those disobeying the nation's regulations or the university disciplinary enactments. The basis of his authority over the members of the nation came from their oath to observe and defend the statutes and privileges of the university and nation, and to obey the rector of the university and the proctor of the nation in all legitimate and honorable demands. The proctor saw to it that students did not live in houses forbidden by the university ban; for example, the houses of landlords who refused to abide by the price-ceiling of rents agreed upon. He was also a judge of first instance with appeal from his decisions to the arts faculty and finally to the university. Like the rector, the proctor received fines for violation of university statutes. The appointment of subordinate officials was not his but belonged to the whole assembly of the nation. Nor could he exceed the instructions for his office, which could be changed only by the nation in its assembly.

One of the proctor's most important duties was calling of and presiding over the nation's assembly, of which he also kept the minutes. There was usually a weekly meeting, and the nation met either at some convent or in its own church. The business was of a varied nature. In view of the monthly term of a proctor, some of the business would concern his election. With each nation conducting its own schools, the maintenance and repair of classrooms also occupied a certain amount of discussion. Each year the French nation, for example, appointed a committee of five masters (one elected by each of the five provinces of the nation) to inspect its schools and to find out who were regent masters and who were not. The report was sent to the proctor, who recorded the names of the regent masters in the nation's record books.

Another matter of business in these assemblies was the election of the two beadles of the nation.[4] Of these, one, the major beadle, ranked next in importance to the proctor and

[4] Cf. Document 3, Appendix.

carried out his commands. Upon election the major beadle took three oaths—to the nation, to the faculty of arts, and to the rector. The sub-beadle took an oath of obedience to the major beadle. The major beadle was in duty bound to carry out the requests of master and proctor and to notify them of the rector's wishes. He aided in keeping order in the schools and announced the various hours for special lectures, the free days, and decisions arrived at in the assemblies. He accompanied the proctor and rector to all assemblies of the faculty and university and stood guard at the door to see that only regent masters or those presenting a special summons were allowed to enter. His salary came from fees paid by the students when they came up for their degrees. The bachelors of the nation also seem to have made some contribution to his collections.

One of the more pleasurable duties of the beadle was his privilege of marching at the head of processions and carrying a silver mace. This mace was his official sign of office. At the end of his yearly term, when he came before the assembled nation, he returned the mace to the proctor with these words: "Lord proctor and masters, here are both your mace and your office of which you may dispose according to your will." Then the nation either voted a renewal of his term or elected another. Upon assuming office, the beadle usually put up a bond as security for the mace which he received. Once when the English nation neglected this safeguard, the widow of their major beadle would not give the mace back to them. Although the nation sued her, they finally had to pay a sum of money to retrieve it.

The official who collected the nations' revenues, the receptor, was chosen for a term of one year either by way of electors selected by the members of the nation, as in the case of the Picard nation, or directly by the assembly itself, as in the Norman nation. Besides collecting fees, he supervised the celebration of the feast days. The nation's revenues came from the fixed fees paid by candidates for degrees and the entrance fees paid by the new members. These entrance fees were not the same for all members, but scaled in accordance with the amount that the entrant swore he paid as his weekly board. Sometimes the entrance fees were increased when the nation had spent more than the usual amount for some feast, repairs of the school, or the like. Another source of reliable revenue came from the fees paid by newly elected officers. (One wonders if this was one reason for the short terms of office.) The receptor held one of the three keys to the nation's treasure box, being present with the other two keyholders when it was opened. The box could only be opened with the express permission of the nation given in an assembly called for that purpose. Each month the receptor had to turn in his financial accounts, and three times a year he presented debts and credits to an assembly called for the purpose. Both receptor and proctor took an oath that they would do this.

Besides the surveillance over schools and masters and the holding of elections of various officials, the assemblies of the nation carefully provided for the special feast days which played a large part in the nation's ordinary life. The images of patron saint or saints were stamped on the nation's seal. In addition to the saints common to the whole university (the Blessed Virgin, St. Nicholas, and St. Catherine), the French nation had as its first patron St. Thomas of Canterbury, and later on St. Guillaume, archbishop of Bourges and a former student of the university. The patron saint of the English nation was St. Edmund, the king and martyr. These feast-day celebrations were not always such as befitted the clerical state or edified the faithful. Simon de Brie, the papal legate, denounced some of their celebrations in severe terms, and in 1276 he threatened with excommunication those who led choruses in the streets, carried weapons, indulged in revelry, or played dice on the church steps.

As regards the academic life of the university, the nations at their assemblies paid heed to the condition of their own schools—their visitation, repair, and sometimes the need for buying other school buildings. Most of the schools were located on the same street, the Rue du Fouarre, "Street of Straw," so named for the straw on which the young pupils in arts sat to hear their masters. In the early fourteenth century it was said that scholars of wealthy families complained when asked to sit on the ground, but Pope Urban V in his reform measures for the university (1366) insisted that this custom should be emphasized as a means of curbing young students' pride. In July, 1387, the papal curia was petitioned, despite the recommendation of Urban V, for permission to put in benches or stools, for it was said that otherwise some of the noble or the more elderly students would not finish their arts course. It is not known whether the request was granted, but in 1452 another set of reforms praised Urban V's ruling and exhorted the university to follow it.

Besides the schools in the Street of Straw, there were some elsewhere. Students could attend any schools or study under any master of their choice. This had been settled in 1249 in one of the earliest recorded disputes. The quarrel originated in the election of a rector, and the other three nations had agreed to forbid their students to attend the schools conducted by the French nation. When peace negotiations were agreed on, the abolition of this measure was one of the conditions, so that the students could have "their wonted freedom to enter the schools of any master whatsoever."

The Nation in the University Assembly

Thus far the four nations at Paris have been considered as separate units, each a corporation with its members, seal, officers, revenues, patron saints, and schools, possessing jurisdiction over its members and inculcating a spirit of loyalty which not infrequently placed devotion to the nation above devotion to the university, or even adherence to common sense. But the nation also played a decisive part in the assembly of the faculties of the whole university. As a member of the assembly, the faculty of arts was one of the four component faculties of the university, and the nations were interested in providing for the things necessary for the arts course in the matter of studies and the various qualifications for the arts degree, as well as for the conferring of the license to teach. When these matters came up for discussion, each nation kept its unity, deliberated apart, and then brought back its decision summed up by the proctor. After these summaries, the rector gave the decision for the whole faculty of arts. The assembly of the faculty of arts was weekly, and only regent masters could attend. In between the meetings the rector and four proctors served as an executive council. The nations also shared in planning the "determination" and the rules and qualifications of the determinants and those to be licensed to teach. As will be noted, this determination was an intellectual exercise in which a student maintained and defended a statement or "thesis" against an opponent. Before 1400 each nation had its own rules for the determiners, who usually took their first degree under a master of their own nation. But as early as 1275 the whole arts faculty had laid down previously enacted rules on the matter of examiners to ensure uniformity in the whole faculty. Three or four examiners were chosen by the nation. After investigating the student's previous scholastic record, they then set up the examination on the prescribed textbooks. Even though the nations chose their examiners privately, these were named in the presence of the university faculty of arts, and immediately took an oath to serve faithfully the interests of the whole faculty and not only their own nation. In the examination for the licentiate each nation sent one examiner, selected not by the nation but by the abbot or chancellor of Ste. Geneviève. This examiner was chosen each month, while the four determinant examiners stayed in office as long as the faculty kept them.

To treat of matters which concerned the university of Paris, and especially to protect its rights and privileges as a corporation, there was a meeting of the whole university, usually on Saturday after the morning Mass either at the church of St. Julien-le-Pauvre or at Mathurins. These proceedings resembled the meetings of the nations or of the faculty of arts as a body. The seven major beadles, one from each of the four nations and one from the faculties of theology, law, and medicine, acted as doorkeepers. Only regent masters dressed in their official garb, or those specially invited, were allowed to enter. The proctor of each nation and the deans of canon law, medicine, and theology were the council, presided over by the rector of the university. Every two years, the provost or mayor of Paris came by royal command to take his oath that he would observe, and would see that others observed, the rights and privileges of the masters and their scholars.

The Rector and the University Assembly

The rector held the highest and most important office of the university. In 1249 the proctors were named as electors of the rector, and in 1274 occurs the first statute naming the rector the head of the arts faculty. He gradually became head of the whole university, although his position was not finally acknowledged until about the middle of the fourteenth century. The dean of theology was seemingly the most reluctant to admit that the head of the arts faculty was also head of the whole university. The proctors, who usually elected the rector, had to take an oath that their choice would be made solely on the basis of the person best fitted for the office and not on a "national" basis. If the vote of the proctors was tied two and two, then the rector could cast a deciding ballot on his successor. If even two proctors could not agree on a man, then four other electors would have to be chosen.

In 1266 Simon de Brie, as papal legate, advocated a longer term for the rector—which up to that time had been only for a month or six weeks. The rector thereafter was elected four times a year either by the proctors or by electors chosen by the nations. The election of the rector was similar to that of a pope in that the four electors were locked in a special room and forbidden to communicate with anyone outside. A candle of specified weight and composition was lit, and they were to finish the election before the light went out. If the candle burned out before they could make up their minds, then four other electors were to be selected, and the voting began again; the process was repeated until some gentleman was finally voted in as rector for his three-month term.

The final word did not rest with the rector but with the university assembly. And in this general congregation each university unit retained its identity. There was no single central organization in the medieval university, but the university itself was a composite of several distinct units. In the university congregation, each nation and faculty had its special place. When the rector, as presiding official, had announced the question for discussion, each faculty and nation withdrew for separate deliberation. On their return, the vote or opinion of each nation or faculty was announced by its proctor or dean. Although the rector summed up the opinions, he did not have a vote. A majority was sufficient for adoption, but the minority opinion was also recorded. A dissident faculty or nation could hold up the proceedings by refusing to affix its own seal to the written enactment.

Each nation had but one vote in the assemblies, regardless of its size. Perhaps in the early history of the university at Paris the principle of "one nation, one vote" was more or less in harmony with the respective numbers of each nation, but later on it was not. In 1439 the English nation had only two masters at the congregation, but it still had one vote. The

French nation, counting a hundred masters, also had one vote. The French nation, decade after decade, protested in vain against this principle; it remained a fundamental axiom at Paris that each nation, regardless of its size, had just one vote.

During the fourteenth and fifteenth centuries the number of foreign scholars considerably diminished. The foundation of many universities in other lands made it unnecessary for students to trek to Paris in order to drink deep of the wells of Aristotle, Gratian, or Galen. Furthermore, the Hundred Years' War (1337–1453) had a disastrous effect on the attendance of the English masters. The Great Western Schism (1378–1417) caused bitter dissensions among the university students and doubtless contributed to the general decline of the foreign student body. When Petrarch, not an unbiased observer, spoke of Paris as he remembered it in 1360, he described a place where one heard "not the sound of disputation but the alarms of war, and saw not stacks of books but stacks of arms." After the battle of Agincourt (1415), it was sadly admitted that there was not a single master in the French nation who had not lost a father, brother, or close friend, and the nation had a solemn requiem Mass celebrated for the repose of their souls.

After the close of the Hundred Years' War, the French monarchy grew in power and authority, and the university lost some of its former independence. In 1474 Louis XI issued an edict against the nominalists, demanding the surrender of books containing such teachings and proscribing a number of masters. The faculty of arts was much offended by this royal measure, and in 1481 the king withdrew his edict. The books were returned to the university, much to the delight of the German nation, many of whose members were nominalists. In

1475 students were sent to the wars despite the privileges of the university, and in 1499 Louis XII took away from the university its great weapon, the privilege of suspending its lectures. A century later (1619) the abolition of the assemblies of nations throughout France was ordered. But the nations themselves lingered on as part of the university organization for another one hundred and seventy-five years until they were completely suppressed by an act of the National Convention of the French Revolution in September, 1793.

NATIONS IN THE UNIVERSITIES OF SOUTHERN EUROPE: THE BOLOGNA PATTERN

In general the universities of southern France, Spain, and Italy copied the form of the nations at Bologna, although in many cases with considerable modification. Padua, Florence, and Orleans are interesting examples of such universities. Some universities in northern Europe, especially those in the Germanies, imitated Bologna. This was also true of those universities which specialized in law.

Padua University began in 1222, founded by students emigrating from Bologna. But in 1228 the students again migrated to Vercelli, where the city fathers offered them better terms than they were getting at Padua. The university came back to Padua again in 1260 and remained there permanently. It gained additional students migrating from Bologna in 1306 and in 1322. Originally, there seem to have been four groups of law students at Padua: the French, Italian, German and Provençal. In the reorganization of 1260, however, these law students were

63

all put into two universities as at Bologna, each with a rector at its head. In the fifteenth century the university had one rector, the cisalpine and transmontane universities taking turns in electing one of their members. Each university was divided into a group of ten nations. The transmontane nations, as tabulated in the 1331 statutes, were the German, Hungarian, Bohemian, Polish, Provençal, Burgundian, Catalonian, Spanish, English-Scotch, and ultramarine; those in the cisalpine university were Rome, Sicily, March of Ancona, Lombardy, Venetia, Dalmatia, Tuscany, March of Treviso, Aquila, and Milan. Every student had to join one of these nations; it mattered not whether he was in canon or civil law. If a student was born in a country not explicitly mentioned, he was enrolled in the nation nearest his birthplace.

Like the students at Bologna, those at Padua elected their *consilarii* from each nation. The nations each had one vote, except for the German nation, which had two, and the English and Scotch, which shared a vote. It would seem that the nations in the universities of Padua did not enjoy as much independence as the Bolognese; but, because we do not have the statutes of the nations before the sixteenth century, this is not certain. The various powers of the rector over the members of the nation seem to indicate that he had more authority than the rector at Bologna. Each student took an oath to obey his rector; if he disobeyed him, he was subject to punishment. The rector alone had the right to decide student quarrels. Any student who dared to appeal the rector's decision to the city court would suffer immediate expulsion. The rector, however, was subject to the majority rule of the university students as expressed in the university congregation made up of the *consilarii* of the various nations, and he was also limited by the statutes drawn up to define his duties and jurisdictions. His duties were much the same as those of the rector at Bologna.

Again like Bologna, Padua developed a separate university for her students in arts and medicine; but they had to wait until 1342 before they were treated as distinct from the law students and until 1360 to obtain the right to elect their own rector. Even then they were bound to take an oath to the rectors of the jurist universities, but in 1399 they finally secured complete separation from the jurist universities. After that time they were subject to their own rector, who was elected by the *consilarii* of the seven nations of the university of arts and medicine, and the official structure of their university paralleled that of the jurist universities.

Another example of a university following the Bologna pattern, but with notable modifications, was that of Florence. A *studium generale* was established at Florence in 1321, modeled after Bologna with two universities of students. But all the transmontane students were grouped into one nation and the cisalpine students put into five other nations. The ultramontane, Tuscan, and Lombard nations had three representatives in the university congregation, while the nations of Rome, Apulia, and March of Ancona had but two. Moreover, the Tuscan nation enrolled the residents of Florence itself. Furthermore, the nations were not purely student organizations but included members of the faculties. The fifteen *consilarii*, or representatives, chosen from the nations named, were apportioned so that the faculties of canon law, civil law, and medicine each had five. The representatives, elected by each nation, had to be over eighteen and from one or more faculties which had members in the nation. The *consilarii* served for a year, without possibility of re-election. Although subject to the rector, they could demand that he submit any question open to discussion for a vote either by ballot or beans. Ten of their number constituted a quorum. The university statutes explained that the reason for the six nations was to prevent any single locality from monopolizing the university offices.

As at Bologna and Padua, the rector was executive head of the university. He was elected annually. Each representative chose an elector from his nation, the rector then added two more, and these seventeen voted for the new rector by written ballots collected by the notary. Whoever received a plurality of votes was elected. The rector had to be a cleric, twenty years of age, unmarried, and not a member of a religious order. To prevent disputes, the rector was elected from the faculties of canon law, civil law, and medicine in turn.

The city of Orleans was famous for its classical school in the twelfth century, but it is not until the first years of the fourteenth century (1306) that a papal document gives us official notice of a university there. The document does not explicitly mention the nations, but the university was given the right to elect a rector and make ordinances and statutes for the conduct of the intellectual guild to be set up. The nations seem to have had their proctors who elected the rector four times a year, and they shared in the enacting of university statutes through these representatives. A bachelor joining the nation took his oath of obedience to his proctor and rector. He promised to come to all the meetings of the university congregation or pay a fine of six *denarii*, to preserve the honor of the nation and university, and to keep secret the doings of the assemblies.

But the students at Orleans were in for hard times. Both the commune and the king of France were much opposed to some of these rights of self-government. The citizens did not want the students to have so much independence and privilege; in 1309 the townsmen dispersed the meeting of the masters at the Dominican church, threatening them with more serious punishment if they did not give up their claim to such independence. The king, wily Philip IV (1285–1314), was not happy about the assemblies of the nations and forbade them because, in his opinion, they fomented division, contributed to disturbance of the peace, and led to riots in which students were injured or even killed. Perhaps the king was influenced by the situation at Paris, where the nations were often embroiled in various fights. Philip de Greve, the chancellor of Paris, bewailed the bellicose attitude of students, declaring that the fights were premeditated and the nations' meetings were used to plan these attacks in advance. He desired the good old days when, according to him, the name of university was unknown, there was more earnestness for study, there was not so much haste, and time was not wasted in so many meetings and discussions.

At any rate Philip IV in December, 1317, declared that the university did not have the right to make its own statutes. But during the same period, the king protected the scholars from the townsmen. In 1310 he forbade the raising of prices of food or lodging, and in 1312 he again emphasized his protection of the students, granting them exemptions from municipal taxes and from the duty of making contributions to the commune. Nevertheless, the university departed for Nevers in 1316 to show its displeasure with both king and commune. Finally the university accepted a compromise agreement by which it would be governed both by a *scholasticus* (like the Paris chancellor) and its own rector, together with a congregation of doctors and the ten proctors of the various nations. At these congregations of the university, presided over by the rector, the members discussed the academic side of the university work, such as the lectures, examinations, courses to be given, time of school year, and the like. At these meetings decisions were reached by a majority vote.

The various nations continued to hold their own assemblies, electing officers and enacting legislation. (The German nation decided not to meet in taverns, the better to avoid brawls.) In fact, the nations at Orleans, apparently becoming more powerful as the fourteenth century progressed, resembled more and more the nations at Paris, each having its own statutes, seals, treasury, feast days, and patron saints. There were frequent denunciations of the student celebrations at Orleans and their useless expenditure of money as each nation tried to outdo the other; in 1365 the university passed a decree to limit the number of feast days which could be celebrated by the various nations. In 1447 Charles VII suggested some reforms for the conduct of their meetings, especially condemning the tumult and noise that hindered the deliberations. No one was to speak until recognized by the presiding officer, and votes must be given distinctly and briefly, in Latin not in French.

With all their independence, the nations at Orleans do not seem to have had much control over the academic side of the university. The meetings of the nations were occupied with election of officers, collections of fees, and plans for the celebrations of festivals. The intellectual side of the student's life —the courses and examinations, the lectures and lecturers, the administration and supervision of the schools—was all taken care of at the university congregations where the nations were represented by their proctors. There was a growing tendency toward centralization, and the university statutes in 1500 demanded that every student take a separate oath of obedience to the rector of the whole university. In 1538 there was a royal edict which reduced the ten nations to four (French, Picard, German, and Norman).

Some of the other universities which in general followed the Bologna pattern were those of Pisa, Ferrara (where the nations were used as indications of the students' original homeland), Perugia (where, however, the commune practically managed the university), and a few in France, such as Poitiers and Angers. Although the Spanish universities were usually created by the king and had students, for the most part, only from the Spanish lands, some of them were divided into nations. Salamanca, founded between 1220 and 1230 by Alfonso IX of León, was an example of this type. The earliest statutes regarding their constitutional arrangement portray a student university patterned after Bologna but with a great majority of Spanish students. According to the statutes, the university at Lérida was a student university with its nations, and the foreign students in canon and civil law had their own student rector chosen by their representatives elected from the various nations. Besides the student rector, however, there was a chancellor appointed by the king. The Spanish universities were more like

69

national institutions brought into existence by royal proclamation and without large bodies of foreign students. Although on paper they appear to have followed the Bologna model in their organization, their problems were really not those of a large cosmopolitan intellectual guild.

THE NATIONS IN THE UNIVERSITIES OF NORTHERN EUROPE: THE PARISIAN STYLE

Just as the universities in the south of Europe generally followed the student-university organization of Bologna, so the universities in northern Europe usually imitated the master-dominated nations of Paris. As with the southern universities, so with the northern, the pattern was subject to many local modifications.

The University of Oxford, coming into recorded history during the second half of the twelfth century, was one of the earliest imitators of Paris. But the system of the four nations was impractical with her small body of Continental students. The nations at Oxford developed into two large groups: the *Boreales*, or the northerners, which included the English students who came from north of the Trent and the Scotch, and the *Australes*, numbering those from south of the Trent as well as Irish, Welsh, and any Latins that might be enrolled.

The two groups often represented the spirit of sectionalism rather than a type of mutual-welfare organization or component part of the university. Their quarrels were fierce and, unfortunately, frequent. For instance, there was a bitter dispute between the Irish students and the northerners in 1252, and later twelve commissioners were selected to draw up the peace terms. Thirty or forty masters from the north and the south guaranteed that the peace would be kept by promising under oath that they would not disturb the order themselves, and that they would discourage trouble-makers from their own or foreign lands. They also promised to bring to the chancellor's notice any information they might have about transgressors in this matter. Each new student entering the university had to take a similar oath. There was another dispute in 1267, and afterwards twenty-four representatives from each group exchanged the kiss of peace. In 1273 there was another fracas in which several Irish scholars were killed; and as the result of an encounter in 1274 four students found themselves lodged by royal order in the Tower of London. Pledges were again exacted and a further oath was laid on each member of the university not to carry weapons. Finally, both nations agreed to unite into one body.

But the old enmities died hard, and there were several brawls during the fourteenth century.

In the early months of the Great Western Schism (1378–1415) there was some dissension, but in 1379 the university agreed to recognize the claims of the Roman line. In 1389 there was a serious dissension which set the Welsh students and the southerners against the *Boreales*. The southerners lost, and the northern students drove the Welsh from the town, firing arrows at them along with their insults. The king and his justices finally brought about peace.

The nations at Oxford always showed that sectionalism

71

which was so strong in the British Isles, and they never seem to have been as influential, either academically or socially, as those at Paris or Bologna.

Each nation had its own proctor, who was chosen annually by indirect election. First two members, one from the northern group and one from the southern, were selected, and these in turn picked six scholars to elect the proctors. The proctors executed the regulations passed in the congregation of the regent masters in arts, and they alone could summon and preside over this congregation. They administered the oaths, kept order and discipline, levied fines, received fees, kept the university's accounts and recorded the expenditures. A chief difference between Oxford and Paris was that Oxford had no rector. Instead, the proctors assisted the chancellor, who at first seems to have represented the bishop of Lincoln. As the university developed, however, the chancellor became the representative of the independence of the university, while still remaining in theory subordinate to the bishop. Nevertheless, the chancellor could be removed from his office by a congregation called by the proctors.

Another university which followed, more or less closely, the Parisian model was that of Prague, established by royal charter of Charles IV in 1348 so that, as was said, his loyal citizens hungry for learning might not be forced to beg alms in foreign countries, but could find set up here in their own kingdom "a table of refreshment." There were four nations at the refreshment table: the Bohemian, Bavarian, Polish, and Saxon. The distribution was based on geographical lines; but, with the exception of the Bohemian, the majority of students in the nations were Germans. These Prague nations included both students and masters, and every member of the university was a member both of a faculty and of a nation. Each nation and each faculty had two *consilarii*, or representatives, on a sixteen-man board which, together with the rector, supervised the university. The choice of these representatives was not by direct balloting; the retiring representatives nominated six from their nation or faculty, and the rector then selected two from each of the six nominees. The nations through their representatives selected various officers, including the rector, who was head of the university, although the jurists from 1372 onwards had a rector of their own.

But the organization of nations foundered on the rocks of growing national consciousness. Antagonism between Bohemians and Germans reached a climax when King Wenceslaus in 1409 ruled that the Bohemian nation would have three votes and the other three nations, formed into one "Teutonic" nation, would have but one. The German nations protested, citing the equality they had always had and the age-old equality of the nations at Paris. All three nations took an oath to migrate from the university if the law was not revoked. The law was not revoked, and migrate they did, many of them ending up at Leipzig University. In the next election for rector at Prague, John Hus was elected, and he immediately proclaimed that since the Germans were not willing to permit the Bohemian nation equality in the universities of Vienna and Heidelberg, they should not take it amiss that the nation of the Bohemians should take first place in the land of the Bohemians.

Although nations were introduced into the various universities of northern Europe after the model of Paris, they were introduced precisely as an imitation of Paris. They did not de-

73

velop from local circumstances, as they had in the early history of the University at Paris. As a result, at some universities they were independent units, but at others they were separate geographical groupings within the university assemblies. In some universities they functioned mainly to elect the rector.

CONCLUSIONS

That there was a great deal of quarreling and disputing between the nations cannot be denied. There was also a fair amount of study time wasted in discussions and contentions in matters that seem rather trivial. On the other hand, the nations had an active life of several centuries—from the beginning of the thirteenth to the end of the eighteenth. Certainly from the thirteenth to the sixteenth century they were influential parts of the university life. For several centuries they performed the duty of educating and examining in some universities, and protecting and defending in all universities, the members of their organization.

More than that, the nations performed another function which, in the long run, may have been one of their most important. They educated the members of their group for a period of six to twelve years (depending on how long it took the scholar to finish both his master of arts and his degree in a higher faculty) in the practical workings of constitutional government. In the nation the member saw his elected executive subjected to a statute constitution and to the will of the majority of the assembly. He was present at the very frequent meetings—far more frequent than any medieval parliament—and he took actual part in close elections conducted by open

74

voting or secret ballot. He was familiar with various devices to prevent election frauds. He witnessed many types of representative government in action, as well as the subordination of one assembly to another in the complicated functioning of the university congregations.

How many of these graduates of the nations' politics found membership in the various committees and councils of kings and princes it is difficult to calculate. When they did—and surely there were many of them so placed at some time or other —they brought to the council table of king, curia or parliament a wealth of actual experience in the functioning of representative government. The history of the influence of the nations of the universities in the gradual development of parliamentary procedures remains to be investigated, but it would not be surprising to find that influence considerable.

ADDITIONAL READINGS

Boyce, Gray C., *The English-German Nation in the University of Paris during the Middle Ages* (Bruges, 1927).

Kibre, P., *Nations in the Mediaeval European Universities*, Mediaeval Academy of America, Publication No. 49 (Cambridge, Mass., 1948). Much of the information in this section (II) has been condensed from this excellent monograph.

Post, Gaines, "Parisian Masters as a Corporation, 1220-1246," *Speculum*, IX (1934), 421-445.

Rashdall, H., Powicke, F. M., Emden, A. B., *The Universities of Europe in the Middle Ages* (Oxford, 1936), 3 vols.

Thorndike, L., *University Records and Life in the Middle Ages*, University of Columbia, Records of Civilization, XXXVIII (New York, 1944).

III. THE CANONIZATION
OF THE TEXTS

During the twelfth century John of Salisbury wrote some descriptive, and caustic, lines about the various educational processes to which he had been subjected.[1] The book he wrote, the *Metalogicon,* is for us a great source of twelfth-century educational materials. John's description makes clear that, although there was considerable study devoted to some of Aristotle's writings, the emphasis on the classical authors and on grammar and rhetoric was by no means slight. John feared that a new, purely pragmatic, type of educational philosophy was gaining influence. He inveighed not so much against the growing emphasis on logical studies as against those who said that a natural ability to argue and discuss, plus a smattering of dialectics, fitted a man for scholarship and teaching. John pleaded for a well-educated scholar, one versed in grammar and literature as well as soundly trained in logic. The Aristotelian writings which were at hand, John praised highly, but the entire Aristotelian corpus of writings was not yet accessible to Western scholars. In the century 1150–1250, European scholars found themselves almost flooded with intellectual materials new to them. On these much of the intellectual life of Europe would feed for centuries.

[1] Cf. *supra,* pp. 12 ff. and Document 1, Appendix.

The twelfth century witnessed one of those rare concurrences of phenomena which historians more easily describe than explain. There had emerged, for example, a cross-breed race of men from barbarian and European stock—the Normans —who wrote their name large across the intellectual, political, and religious history of France, England, Sicily, and southern Italy. There arose the communes with their merchant and craft guilds, winning their independence from the feudal society which gave in sometimes graciously and sometimes grudgingly. During these same decades feudal monarchs slowly transformed their monarchies, groping toward the centralized states of later centuries. These were some of the environmental circumstances which aided and abetted the growth of a new intellectual culture such as Europe had not yet seen. It was rude and strong, almost barbaric in its rough intensity; but Christian in a way that previous cultures, adapted to or adopted by Christianity, could not or would not be.

It is true that much of the material which so influenced the development of medieval studies was not new in itself; but it was certainly new to the medieval Europeans. The effect of this "discovery" of the Aristotelian body of writings on the intellectual world was comparable in a certain sense to that of the discovery of America centuries later on the economic and geographic world. It set philosophers thinking as they had not thought before, and it gave the arts course in the universities a new development and special emphasis. But it was not only in philosophy that great works opened before medieval eyes; for during these same decades the medical work of Galen, of Hippocrates, and of Avicenna became the joy of medical students all over Western Europe, and the vast resources of Roman law in the volumes of the *Digest,* and the collection of

77

canon law in the *Decretum* of Gratian, formed the curricula of the faculties of canon and civil laws. Theology, which, at Paris at least, was regarded as the queen of the sciences, was blessed too with the systematized work of Peter Lombard, the *Sentences*, which, together with the Bible, became the textbook for the faculty of theology from the late twelfth until the sixteenth century.

The sudden discovery of so much intellectual material in so relatively short a time (1150–1250) evoked an enthusiasm for study and brought thousands of students to the newly formed universities. It is true that the books of the seven liberal arts were still used and taught and that grammar (albeit a more philosophical grammar) was still expounded in the arts at Paris. It is also true that there were other works brought in from the Arabic world, treatises in mathematics and philosophy. But the vast collections just named formed the basic intellectual staple of these universities for several centuries. Some general idea of what these collections contained is necessary if one is to understand anything about medieval university life.

THE BOOKS STUDIED IN THE UNIVERSITY ARTS COURSE

The twelfth century had witnessed an increasing emphasis on the study of logic within the framework of the seven liberal arts. During the thirteenth and fourteenth centuries, philosophical studies played a more and more preponderant part in the medieval arts course. Oxford and some of the German universities retained parts of the *trivium* and *quadrivium,* and rhetoric was an important study in Italy, but all in all the story of the arts course during these centuries was largely the story of the spread of, and overwhelming interest in, the works of Aristotle.

Aristotle's books represented a veritable encyclopedia of knowledge and were the product of a teacher who has been acclaimed by succeeding generations as one of mankind's greatest intellectual geniuses. The various Aristotelian books practically all came from the period 335–322 B.C., and can be divided into three large groups. First, there are several treatises which are known as the *Organum,* and they include *The Categories, On Interpretation, Prior Analytics, Posterior Analytics, Topics,* and *On Sophistical Refutations.* This group of writings dealt with logic, and more especially with an exhaustive treatment of the syllogism (*Prior Analytics*) and an analysis of demonstration or proof (*Posterior Analytics*). The simplest way for the student to understand what the medieval "artist" (as students in the arts course were called) studied and became enthusiastic about is to take a translation of some of Aristotle's works and page down the table of contents, select some topic that interests him and read a few pages about it. He may find the going a bit rough. But he will gain a first-hand experience with medieval textbooks that no amount of description could give him.[2]

A second group of works treated of "natural philosophy"; for example, theories of the universe (*On the Heavens*), theories of motion, time, and place (*Physics*), tractates in biology (*On Parts of Animals, Locomotion of Animals, Gener-*

[2] The edition by R. McKeon, *Basic Works of Aristotle* (New York; Random House, 1941), offers easy access to these medieval textbooks.

79

ation of Animals), and books discussing what today is called experimental and rational psychology, as well as books on *Metaphysics*.

A third group of Aristotelian writings delved profoundly into problems of human conduct, human government, and literature, the *Ethics, Politics, Rhetoric,* and *Poetics*. Again a sampling of some of these sections would provide the best way to gain an idea of what the medieval student worked on and studied; for instance, the second and third books of the *Ethics* on the idea of virtue, or the fifth book (in our editions today) of the *Politics* on "Revolutions" should prove interesting.

This vast amount of material was not made available all at once but over a period of decades. John of Salisbury, writing in the middle of the twelfth century, could not know of the *Politics*, which St. Thomas Aquinas commented on some time shortly after the second quarter of the thirteenth century. These different Aristotelian works found their way into the medieval arts curriculum during the thirteenth century in ever increasing numbers, so that by the last quarter of that century the Aristotelian corpus, or body of writings, was fully at the disposal of the medieval professors and students.

To help us measure the progress of this increasing emphasis on philosophy, and especially on logic, in the arts course, there are some helpful documents; not many, it must be admitted, but some at least, and these from the University of Paris, so important because it was the model for many other universities. The first document to consider is the rule of studies drawn up by the cardinal legate, Robert de Courçon, for the University of Paris in the year 1215.[3] In the decree the arts course is

[3] Cf. Document 2, Appendix.

described as made up of lectures on the "old and new dialectic" —that is to say, on the *Organum* of Aristotle. This is the course of studies for the artists in the "ordinary" lectures. These "ordinary" lectures were those given in the morning hours, at which, it would seem, a more thorough treatment was given than in the other type of lecture named "extraordinary" at Bologna and "cursory" at Paris.[4] Besides the staple diet of logical treatises, the books of the "two Priscians" are added. These were eighteen treatises on the study of Latin grammar, the *Institutio grammatica*, by Priscian, a fifth-century Latin writer.

On the festival days the artists could attend lectures on the philosophers, on rhetoric, on subjects of the *quadrivium* (i.e., arithmetic, geometry, music and astronomy), on *Barbarismus* (the third book of the *Ars Maior* of the Latin grammarian Donatus, who taught St. Jerome), as well as lectures on Aristotle's *Ethics* (this then meant the first three books in what we call the *Nicomachean Ethics* of Aristotle), and the fourth book of the *Topics*. With regard to the *Ethics*, students could attend lectures "if it pleased them"; while with the others, it was said that they could not have any lectures on feast days except on the subjects mentioned. There were between sixty and one hundred holidays during the medieval university calendar year, and so the extraordinary, or cursory, lectures were by no means to be overlooked in estimating the amount of materials in the medieval curriculum. Even at this early stage (1215), however, the core of the arts course is evidently the *Organum* of Aristotle. The decree forbids public lectures on the Aristotelian *Metaphysics* and *Natural Philosophy* or summaries of them, and another decree in 1231 again forbids those books "on

4 Cf. a fuller explanation of class schedules *infra*, pp. 108 ff.

81

nature which were forbidden by the provincial council for certain reasons, until they shall have been examined and expurgated."[5]

This prohibition of important works of that thinker who soon became, for the medieval philosophers and theologians, "the master of them that know" should not come as too much of a surprise. Certain doctrines in Aristotle's writings did not harmonize with Christian revelation: namely, his judgments concerning the eternity of the world, the immortality of the soul in relation to his theories on the two intellects—one "passive and perishable" and the other active but impersonal—and lastly, his concept of a Supreme Being who took little account of the world and the men in it.[6] For Christians in their teens who believed in a non-eternal world, in an immortal personal soul, and in a God deeply interested in them, Aristotle could be a dangerous companion. Perhaps for reasons like this,[7] the bishops of the dioceses near Paris met in a local synod and decided to forbid "books of Aristotle on natural philosophy and their commentaries to be lectured on at Paris in public or private," and they threatened anyone who disobeyed the order with excommunication, that is, with exclusion from the Church. In 1215 the cardinal legate, Robert de Courçon, whose decree we have mentioned above, excluded the actual public class lectures on the materials. On April 23, 1231, Pope Gregory IX, who had been a student at Paris, wrote as follows:

[5] Cf. document in Thorndike, *Univ. Records*, pp. 35–39.

[6] Some of the earlier translations of Aristotle's works had made a long trek from Greek to Syrian to Arabic to a Spanish dialect and then to medieval Latin. The trip was frequently hard on the original.

[7] How much influence the Augustinian theologians and the conservative element brought to bear in this matter is not known clearly.

82

Since, as we have learned, the books on nature, which were prohibited at Paris in provincial council, are said to contain both useful and useless matter, lest the useful be vitiated by the useless, we command your discretion, in which we have full faith in the Lord, firmly bidding by apostolic writings, under solemn adjuration of divine judgment, that examining the same books as is convenient subtly and prudently, you entirely exclude what you shall find there erroneous or likely to give scandal or offense to readers, so that what are suspect being removed, the rest may be studied without delay and without offense. . . . Given at the Lateran, April 23, in the fifth year of our pontificate.[8]

In 1255 another document was drawn up concerning the courses in arts for Paris. The arts curriculum was very heavily weighted in favor of Aristotle.[9] The very books forbidden by the provincial synod some forty years before now formed part of the ordinary lecture materials. In fact, to the Aristotelian works found in the 1215 document there are added the *Physics*, *Metaphysics*, *On the Soul*, *On Animals*, *On the Heavens*, *On Generation and Corruption*, *Meteorology*, *On Sense and Sensible* (perceptible) *Things*, *On Memory and Remembering*, *On Sleep and Waking*, *On Life and Death*. A treatise *On Plants*, thought to be spurious, and the *Six Principles* of Gilbert de la Porrée (a commentary on Aristotle's *Categories*), the *Two Priscians* and another little work of Priscian, *On Accent*, are also to be included. The decree gives a good general idea of the medieval collegiate textbooks, for Paris was the model most ordinarily followed in the arts curriculum.

[8] Reprinted with permission from Lynn Thorndike, *University Records and Life in the Middle Ages* (New York: Columbia University Press, 1944), Document 20, p. 40.
[9] Cf. Document 4, Appendix.

A century later there is another group of statutes made for the university of Paris, called the "Reform Statutes of 1366."[10] This list takes the books and divides them into the groups to be taken by the student in arts as he progresses from bachelor to licentiate to master in arts.[11] As a bachelor he studied grammar, logic and psychology in practically the same books as were numbered in 1255, except that instead of the *Two Priscians* we now find the *Grecismus* of Eberhard and a grammar by Alexander of Villedieu, the *Doctrinale*, written in verse, which was *the* textbook in grammar until the sixteenth century. In addition, the bachelor of arts had to master the *Organum*, as in previous decrees, and the work *On the Soul*. For the licentiate there were the other works of Aristotle on "natural philosophy" enumerated above, and the *Metaphysics*, together with some mathematical works. Between the time of obtaining his license to teach and his inception as a master of arts, the applicant had to master the *Ethics* and three books of the *Meteorology*.

The last group of statutes to be noted in the various developments and reforms of the Paris art faculty were drafted another century later (1452). Practically no change is made in the curriculum with the exception of some emphasis on versification. This may perhaps indicate the influence of the humanists making a small dent in the Aristotelian armor. Viewed in the large, however, there is no doubt that the arts curriculum was centered on philosophy and that the medieval faculty of arts would today be more properly called a faculty of philosophy.

A comparison of this medieval course of arts with a conserv-

[10] Cf. document in Thorndike, *Univ. Records*, pp. 244–247.
[11] These terms are more fully explained *infra*, pp. 125 ff.

ative American arts college B.A. is interesting. In the example chosen the total of credit hours required for a B.A. is 128, one hour being equal to one hour of class study for a semester. The division breaks down to this: English and other languages, about 40 hours; science, 8 hours; history, 6 hours; philosophy, 20 hours; field of major concentration (this might be science, history, etc.), 30 hours; plus several hours of electives. The effects of the humanistic and later educational movements and theories can be clearly seen in the modern curriculum.

The above comparison also shows how large a part the study of Aristotelian philosophy played in the medieval arts course. This does not mean that at some places there was not more time given to literary studies than might be true at Paris. But, by and large, the arts course for the medieval university gave much less emphasis to literary studies than does its modern counterpart. It should also be mentioned that in addition to the actual works of Aristotle listed in the decrees there were other minor works studied. For example, the summary textbook in logic of Peter of Spain—afterwards Pope John XXI (1276–1277)—was a popular text for several centuries, as was the *Parva Logicalia* of Marsilius of Inghen. Other works of Aristotle that apparently were mastered but were not mentioned in the documents were the *Politics*, the *Economics* and the *Rhetoric*.

Thus, although there were some students and university masters who continued the classical tradition, a comparison of John of Salisbury's description of his own education in the first half of the twelfth century with that of the Parisian statutes for the thirteenth and fourteenth seems to indicate that, generally speaking, the study of Ovid and Vergil largely ceased

85

when the student left his cathedral school for university work.

LAW BOOKS AND LAW CODES

As Paris spearheaded the development of the medieval arts course, so in the matter of law Bologna is the place of influence. And it is interesting to find, as was noted above,[12] that at Bologna the two great founts of law studies were organized and systematized during the same century and that each was influenced greatly by a single individual—Irnerius for civil, and Gratian for canon, law.

The books used in the study of civil law were the Roman law books. Up to the time of Justinian's great series of collections (edited between A.D. 529 and 533), Roman law had grown into a tremendous mass of legal material. This accumulation had come from the equity decisions of magistrates, from the praetors' edicts for private law, to which were added the arrangements and the rationalizations of great Roman legal thinkers, men like Papinian, Gaius, Ulpian, Paul, and Modestinus. In addition there were the decrees of the emperors over hundreds of years—and with not a few contradictions! The Theodosian code had dispelled some of the obscurity for the Western part of the empire. Still, the great mass of Roman law, although unquestionably monumental, resembled in many ways the inside of a vast disorganized antique shop. On these materials Justinian put to work the best jurists he could find.

First, they produced the *Code* in twelve volumes, containing the statutes of the emperors from A.D. 200 to Justinian's time. In the preface to the *Digest*, Justinian remarks that since they

[12] Cf. pp. 24 ff.

had found the statutes of the emperors to be in an infinite state of confusion they had decided to start with them and put them in order first, so that they could be collected into one volume. The second section of the collection was named the *Digest* or *Pandects* and was a work of some *fifty* volumes. Justinian said that he had given the "whole task to Tribonian, a most distinguished person, Master of the Offices, and ex-quaestor of the Sacred Palace and ex-consul . . . so that together with other well-known and learned colleagues he might bring it to accomplishment." Justinian also remarked that Tribonian had pointed out to him that there were some two thousand books written by the old lawyers with some three million lines to read and ponder. From this Tribonian put together his "condensation" of fifty volumes. In medieval works the *Digest* was cited under three heads: the *Digestum Vetus* ("Old Digest"), the *Infortiatum* (about books 24 to 38), and the *Digestum Novum* ("New Digest"), perhaps because they were found thus separated in the manuscript copies that came into the hands of the medieval researchers. The third part of the collection was the *Institutes*, and Justinian described it as a collection of books in which "a brief exposé is given of the ancient laws" (collected in the *Digest*) and also "from the commentaries of Gaius . . . and also from many other commentaries." These four books of the *Institutes* were to be considered elementary texts in the study of Roman law, in order that the student "may no more learn the first elements from old and erroneous sources but learn them by the clear light of imperial wisdom; so that, although formerly young students could hardly after three years of study read the imperial constitutions, they may now begin their studies by reading them." Justinian further hoped that when the students' course of legal study was finished they might "govern our empire in the different portions entrusted to their care." Another section of the Code, called the *Novellae* ("Novels"), was issued from 536 to 565; these were new statutes but not officially collected.

Although the *Code* and *Institutes* were known during the darkest period of the ninth and tenth centuries, the *Digest* does not seem to have been known in Western Europe from the sixth to the eleventh centuries. It was this vast collection which Irnerius used to such great advantage in the eleventh century and which had much the same exhilarating effect on the legal intelligence that the various discoveries of the Aristotelian works had on the lovers of philosophy.

Canon law, too, had its great scholar. About 1140 a hitherto little-known monk of the Camaldolese, or Benedictine, monastery of Sts. Felix and Nabor at Bologna issued a work which placed the study of canon law upon a new footing. Before Gratian's time there had been collections of canon-law materials—that is to say, of the laws passed by Church councils and of the decrees of the popes—but these collections were incomplete and poorly arranged, and they contained contradictory materials and decisions. The state of Church law at this time resembled in a striking way the situation of Roman law when Justinian directed his corps of legal experts to the problem. Gratian was but one man, but he was able to put forth a canon-law code in his new *Decretum*, or *Concordantia discordantium canonum*. It was a masterful collection containing some 3,900 canons, or chapters, and was divided into three main parts. In general, in the first part, Gratian discussed laws of divine and human origins, or from another viewpoint ec-

88

clesiastical persons and duties; in part two, he treated of judgments, civil and criminal cases; in part three, of some of the sacraments and sacramentals.

However, his work was not merely a collection. More exactly, it was a series of treatises setting forth the opinions of others as well as his own. Gratian argues from intrinsic reasons —that is, he uses the canons, the judgments of the Fathers of the Church, the decretals, and the like. Although he did not avoid all confusion, Gratian produced much more order than had existed before. His work in harmonizing discordant opinions and in putting at the disposal of students a far more complete collection than had existed before has brought him the name of the founder of the scientific study of canon law. As other professors taught from Gratian's collection in later decades, they added their own notes, sometimes between the lines (interlinear glosses) or on the margin (marginal notes or glosses). Some authors put together the works of various glossators so as to form a continuous commentary on the text. The one produced by Bartholomew about 1250 became the standard commentary on the text and was called the *glossae ordinariae* ("ordinary glosses"). There were further additions to Gratian's material during the succeeding centuries, mainly four other collections: (1) the *Decretales* ("Decretals"), in five books, published by Pope Gregory IX in 1234; the *Liber Sextus* ("Sixth Book"), edited as a supplement to the *Decretales* by Pope Boniface VIII in 1298; the *Constitutiones Clementinae* ("Constitutions of Clementine"), in 1317; and a collection of several sets of papal laws known as the *Extravagantes*.

Sometimes students bring about the writing of textbooks by their professors, but in the case of Gratian and canon law, it

89

was the other way around. Not only did Gratian's *Decretum* bring together a tremendous number of law students, but it may be said that by his work he went far to create the ecclesiastical—or canon—law faculties in the various universities from his day down to our own.

MEDICAL KNOWLEDGE IN A PLASTER CAST

The curriculum and the teaching techniques of the medical faculties in the medieval universities form one of the more difficult problems for a modern student to grasp and understand. Medieval theology and canon law were themselves Christian things; civil law, coming under a Latin imperial dress, was Christianized in part at least; while philosophy, basically Aristotelian, was also modified by Christian thinkers. Medicine, however, was largely a Greek contribution, and even in its Latin translations it was memorized rather than modified. Generally, the basic textbooks were the works of either Hippocrates or Galen, and a word should be said about both men since their names were writ so large across the brow of medieval medical science.

Hippocrates, called the greatest practitioner of his art, lived during the great age of Greece when Pericles was guiding the destinies of Athens, while Herodotus and Thucydides set ideals for future historians, and Greek dramatists achieved their masterpieces. Born about 460 B.C. on the tiny island of Cos, Hippocrates lived out a long old age, dying, according to some, at the age of one hundred and four. He studied under his father, who was a doctor, and seems to have traveled extensively—although, apparently, he never visited Athens. Legends formed about his name, but one thing is certain: he left an extensive body of medical writings which have formed the basis of his influence throughout the ages. Modern scholars generally credit him with some *seventy-two* books discussing about fifty different subjects and written in Ionic Greek. Our oldest copies go back only to the tenth century. The books of Hippocrates have been commented on and translated into various languages; there is, for instance, a four-volume set in English.[13] Some of the titles of the works which he wrote give us an indication of the genius of the man and the breadth of his knowledge in an age when medicine was in its infancy. He edited treatises on *Anatomy, On the Nature of the Bones, On the Humors, On the Seventh-Month Fetus, On Fractures, On Fistulas, On Injuries of the Head,* etc. The "Oath of Hippocrates," even if not actually written by him, is certainly indicative of his spirit and ideals.[14] Three characteristics of this oath are worth noting: the prohibition of practicing abortion, the duty of the doctor not to advise, allow, or commit any act prejudicial to his patient's health, and, finally, the clear concept of professional secrecy.

Hippocrates, in common with the teaching of his day, regarded the body as formed of the four elements—air, earth, water, and fire. Each of these had its particular quality—cold, hot, dry, or wet. The humoral concept played an essential part

[13] *Hippocrates,* Loeb Classical Series, with the Greek text and the English translation, edited by W. H. S. Jones and E. T. Withington (1923–1931).

[14] Cf. the translation in A. Castiglioni, *A History of Medicine,* trans. by E. B. Krumbhaar (New York: Alfred A. Knopf, 1947), p. 154.

in his theories, as can be gathered from his remarks in his treatise *On the Nature of Man*.[15] Hence the so-called sympathy of the various parts of the organs was stressed. Everything is founded on a union of the humors, a united concordance and sympathy. It is on these principles that the purgative treatments of spring and fall and some revulsive remedies in favor for some twenty-five hundred years were all based. It is difficult to summarize even the outlines of the multitudinous treatises penned by Hippocrates or his pupils, but they dominated medicine for many centuries. Briefly, Hippocratic medicine was based on what was then known of the natural sciences plus a wide experience in practical medicine. Added to these was the constant use of logical reasoning from cause to effect, joined to an ethical concept based on a moral law. It has been said that "Hippocratic medicine, founded essentially on bedside experience and philosophic reasoning, succeeded in rising to heights that have seldom been surpassed," and this in spite of "faulty knowledge of anatomy, physiology and pathology, and in spite of the poverty of animal investigations, seldom and but crudely attempted."

Claudius Galen (A.D. 138–201), a Greek from Pergamon in Asia Minor, was another of the great authors whom medieval doctors followed. He came on the scene when medicine was more or less stereotyped, when the various schools, which arose after the death of Hippocrates, had become static, when medicine frequently degenerated into long theoretical controversies based on theory and not on observation or experience. Galen was a lifelong student, writer, and observer. After ex-

15 In ch. 4 (pp. 11–12) of the Jones-Withington translation referred to above.

tensive travels, he transferred his practice to Rome, where he soon became the outstanding doctor of the Roman world. His writings appear to have numbered more than four hundred treatises, of which we still have about eighty surely authentic and twenty more doubtful, plus some fifteen commentaries on Hippocratic works. Galen was a gifted physician who united to his own observations all that he could extract from the writings of Hippocrates. Unfortunately, he was a man absolutely sure of himself, a born dogmatist who knew all the answers and promptly wrote them down! He knew animal anatomy better than anyone before him; but he transferred his results, without qualification, to humans. His masterly analyses satisfied those who came after him; his confident answers were regarded as almost infallible by too many; while the very spirit of observation which resulted in some of his best accomplishments was lost in the halo of authority that gradually transformed his work into a marble-like structure, beautiful but unchangeable.

In the centuries that followed the breakup of the Roman Empire and the Roman system of administration, medicine, like many other elements of Western culture, found refuge in the monasteries. Preserving the actual texts of the medical literature of the age by patiently copying them, Cassiodorus and his successors educated their monks in the value of the study of the Latin translations of Galen and Hippocrates. In addition, the growth and development of the hospital or infirmary under monastic or clerical help and supervision aided greatly the continuity of medical practice. The great Benedictine abbey of Montecassino played an important part in this conservation of medical knowledge.

Before the actual university work in medicine, there was a famous medical school at Salerno. Although there is no clear historical foundation for the story that Salerno owes its existence to four physicians, a Greek, a Latin, a Jew, and a Saracen, the legend does point up the various currents of medical opinion that found their way into its making. Salerno, mentioned as early as the ninth century, reached its zenith in the twelfth, and it was during this time that Arabian medicine showed its greatest influence there, especially through the work of an indefatigable translator, Constantinus Africanus.

Constantinus was born in Carthage (hence the name Africanus) and devoted himself from his earliest years to the study of medicine. After several years at Salerno, he joined the Benedictine community at Montecassino, where he spent the remainder of his life, dying there in 1087. He was always translating something; writings continually poured from his cell. He reminds one of some of the humanists of the Renaissance, a scholarly man with a knowledge of languages that others about him did not possess, gifted with an energy that never let itself rest. To him, and to the men who imitated him later on, medical knowledge in the West is in deep debt.

Although in these earlier centuries at Salerno there were gifted doctors, vivid interest in things medical, and writings of medical men both in old and new translations, there was no university. Not until the thirteenth century does Salerno become a true university, and by then her years of unique glory are past. The universities of Montpellier and Bologna are the places where the medieval university faculty of medicine forms one of the faculties of the university guild of students, training

94

its members from apprentice to master like the other faculties.[16] Using the main works of Galen and Hippocrates and the Arabian doctor Avicenna, the medieval university faculty of medicine trained its medical students. Surgery was often considered a subject apart from university medical training. Although anatomy of the human body was studied by means of the actual dissection of a human cadaver, such proceedings were relatively rare—one or two a year in the faculty, and attendance necessarily limited by this fact. Generally, it would seem that the actual anatomy studied was rigorously imitative of what had been written in the great classics, with the professor conducting the anatomical dissection, pointing out, book in hand, the various sections of the cadaver.[17]

Nevertheless during these centuries there were outstanding doctors and surgeons, many of whom made notable contributions to the progress of medical science. An example is Master Taddeo Alderotti, a Florentine, who taught at the University of Bologna in the second half of the thirteenth century. A close follower of Aristotelian maxims, he has been called the real founder of dialectical medicine. He wrote commentaries on Hippocrates much as the lawyers wrote commentaries on Justinian's codes. In these he followed a new type of medical literature, the *consilia*, or collections of clinical cases. During the heyday of scholastic methods in medical education, these *consilia* introduced a needed practical note. Taddeo also wrote, in Italian, a popular book on the care of one's health, of which this is a typical citation:

[16] Cf. document in Thorndike, *Univ. Records*, pp. 81–82.
[17] Cf. document in Thorndike, *Univ. Records*, pp. 283–284.

When you get up each morning, stretch your limbs; nature is comforted thereby, the natural heat is stimulated and the limbs strengthened. Then comb your hair, as the combing removes uncleanliness and comforts the brain. Wash your hands and face also with cold water to give your skin a good color and to stimulate natural heat. Wash and clean your nose and your chest by expectorating and also clean your teeth, because the stomach and the chest are aided thereby and your speech becomes clearer. Clean your teeth and your gums with the bark of some odoriferous tree. From time to time fumigate your brain with precious spices; in hot weather use cold things like sandalwood; when it is cold use hot things like cinnamon, cloves, myrrh, the wood of aloes and similar articles. This thorough fumigation will open your nostrils and your brain, will keep your hair from degenerating and becoming white and will keep the face plump. Adorn your body with fine clothing, as the spirit is rejoiced thereby; and chew fennel, anise, cloves, because this strengthens the stomach, gives a good appetite and sweetens the breath; again, use the following things to suppress the vapours and melancholy; daisies, new amber rose, clove pinks and similar articles. After that, exercise your body as you are accustomed, though in moderation, because fatigue has many virtues; it stimulates the natural heat and burns up superfluities before eating.[18]

A famous thirteenth-century surgeon was the Dominican Friar Theodore of Lucca (1205–1298), bishop first of Bitonto and then of Cervia. He has the merit of being one of those who fought against the theory which declared dogmatically that the formation of pus was necessary for the healing of wounds, and also was one of the first to use simple drugs for their treat-

[18] A. Castiglioni, *A History of Medicine*, trans. by E. B. Krumbhaar (New York: Alfred A. Knopf, 1947), pp. 334–335.

ment, declaring that the complicated prescriptions in customary use were really obstacles to healing. He recommended the application of wine as the best method of healing wounds. In one of his books Theodore described the use of narcotics to put the patient to sleep before surgery; sponges were drenched with a narcotic such as opium, mandragora, or jusquiamus, then dried out and kept ready for use; immediately before use, they were soaked in hot water, and the patient was instructed to breathe deeply as they were held to his nose.

Another important medical man of the thirteenth century was the Milanese Guido Lanfranchi (Lanfranc), who did much to introduce surgery into France. Exiled by the Visconti he went to Lyons and then to Paris. His *Chirurgia Magna* (1296) became a standard text at the University of Paris. A cautious surgeon, he preferred cautery to the knife, but he was an acute observer and a skilful operator. His observations on fracture of the skull and the symptoms it produces, as well as the indications he gives for trephining, the types of bandages he recommends for hernias, and his remarks on lithotomy, are proofs of this. Lanfranc's description of the qualifications of a surgeon are interesting:

It is necessary that a surgeon should have well-formed hands, long slender fingers, a strong body, not inclined to tremble, with all his members trained to the capable fulfillment of the wishes of his mind. He should be of deep intelligence and of a simple, humble, brave but not audacious disposition. He should be well grounded in natural science and should know not only medicine but every part of philosophy; should know logic well, so as to be able to understand what is written, to talk properly and to support what he has to say by good reasons.

97

And he added this piece of advice:

The surgeon should not love difficult cases and should not allow himself to be tempted to undertake those that are desperate. He ought to help the poor as far as he can, but he should not hesitate to ask for good fees from the rich.[19]

Lanfranc advocated the union of surgery with medicine, pointing out that no one could be a good doctor unless he knew surgery, and no one a good surgeon unless he knew medicine.

Perhaps the greatest of the medieval surgeons and doctors was the French physician Guy de Chauliac, who first took his doctorate in medicine from the famous school of Montpellier and then went down to Italy for post-graduate work, for fourteenth-century Italy was regarded as the intellectual and scientific leader of Europe. After long years of scholarly training, Guy produced his textbook of surgery, *Chirurgia Magna*. Succeeding generations have praised the quality of his work. Guy stressed the importance of a knowledge of anatomy, which he had learned from the many anatomical dissections he had witnessed. He thus described the teaching of his master, Bertruccius of Bologna: "The dead body having been placed on a bench, he used to make four lessons on it; in the first, the nutritional portions were treated, because they are so likely to become putrefied; in the second, he demonstrated the spiritual members; in the third, the animate members; in the fourth, the extremities." His remarks on certain previously written surgical works were at times quite blunt:

[19] James J. Walsh, *Old Time Makers of Medicine* (New York: Fordham University Press, 1911), pp. 261–262.

One thing particularly is a source of annoyance to me . . . that (these writers) follow one another like so many cranes. For one always says what the other says. . . . They have, to my mind, understood very badly Aristotle's second book of the *Metaphysics* where he shows that these two things, fear and love, are the greatest obstacles on the road to the truth. Let them give up such friendship and fears, "because while Socrates or Plato may be a friend, truth is a greater friend." Truth is a holy thing and worthy to be honored above everything else. Let them follow the doctrine of Galen, which is entirely made up of experience and reason and in which one investigates things and despises words.[20]

His descriptions of various surgical operations, especially in regard to the three "dreaded cavities" of the human body (the skull, thorax, and abdomen) were remarkable. He discussed the use of anaesthesia for amputations and was aware of the necessity of antisepsis in surgery. His emphasis on the use of stronger wine as a dressing, and on cleanliness during the operation, made possible the success of surgery that would have been fatal otherwise. Unfortunately, the importance of these observations was not recognized, and other doctors turned back to the theory of "laudable pus" and the necessity of provoking it for a healing process. Guy spent the last twenty-five years of his life as papal physician at Avignon for Clement VI (1342–1352), Innocent VI (1352–1362), and Urban V (1362–1370). He was present in Avignon when the Black Death struck, and he remained with heroic courage to tend the dying. While denouncing those doctors who fled the city, he admitted with characteristic humility that though he stayed and risked his life, he was ever in fear of the disease. At last he did contract

[20] Walsh, *op. cit.*, p. 292.

it, and for a time his life was despaired of, but finally he re-recovered and lived on until about 1370.

Though some doctors evidently ran away from the cities when the merciless Black Death snatched away probably almost one-third of all Europe's people within a few years, modern medical men can be proud of the record of the medical profession of the fourteenth century as a group. Possibly no body of medical men in history ever had to face such a terrible unknown and deadly plague. Courageously visiting their patients, many doctors gave their lives in what must have seemed a hopeless situation, contracting and dying of a disease that was as swift as it was incurable by any of their remedies. But they set a high standard for the medical profession. The fact that Guy de Chauliac had himself measured up to that ideal adds weight to his description of the good surgeon:

The surgeon should be learned, skilled, ingenious and of good morals. Be bold in things that are sure, cautious in dangers; avoid evil cures and practices; be gracious to the sick, obliging to his colleagues, wise in his predictions. Be chaste, sober, pitiful and merciful; not covetous nor extortionate of money; but let the recompense be moderate, according to the work, the means of the sick, the character of the issue or event, and its dignity.[21]

From the history and work of men like these, it is evident that there were outstanding doctors during these centuries, medical men who would not be bound by the letter but followed the spirit of the classical authors. Going beyond the mere form of the textbook, they made discoveries of their own, and their works remained key sources of information

[21] Walsh, *op. cit.*, p. 305.

100

alongside those of the earlier Greek and Arabian physicians. Still, it would seem that they were the exceptions and that their spirit did not go marching on. Original thinking in any generation is a rare achievement, but in medical matters during the thirteenth and fourteenth centuries it seems to have been at a premium. Generally, the average university training was a book knowledge of medicine, and the whole science of medicine was handled in exactly the same fashion as the *Physics* of Aristotle. Men of that era saw no reason why the methods so successful in the study of law, philosophy, and theology should not be applied to medicine. Thus there developed an abstract type of medical training, composed of a whole body of reasoned conclusions in which the various medical problems were treated as if they were problems in metaphysics. They were analyzed and organized, discussed and disputed, both in the classroom and in the times set aside for formal disputations. We find the medical student following the methods of the artist, the theologian, the civil or canonical lawyer. He learned how to argue and analyze the masters whose principles he memorized; but of actual experimental knowledge there was an unfortunate lack. Many of the conclusions were logical and clear, but they were also wrong. There was nothing erroneous about the logic, but the premises were often based on insufficient evidence, and they were not verified or codified by continual testing of experimental procedures.[22]

As a result the classroom medicine of the period tended to become more and more a great body of organized medical knowledge, much of which was good, some of which was

[22] For a sample medical curriculum cf. document in Thorndike, *Univ. Records*, pp. 280–281.

erroneous, but all of which was solidly imbedded in a plaster cast of ancient authorities. When this has been said, the worst criticism against the medieval university medical faculty has been made. But what is sometimes overlooked is the cardinal fact that the medieval university established *a body of regulations* and *a tradition of medical education* of the greatest importance. The medieval medical student spent some eight or nine years in his course, five years after his licentiate in arts, or six if he did not have the license, according to the Paris regulations of 1272. This insistence on a specialized training conducted in a standardized way under a body of organized teachers was of the greatest importance for the future of medical education. When the conservatism of these faculties of medicine was broken through, when the newer findings of reasoned experiments supplanted mere theory, then the universities provided that tradition of medical education which, combined with the surer medical knowledge based on accurate anatomy, produced the European (and American) doctor, a *university man* trained in medicine and surgery.

Sixteen Years for a Ph.D.: The Doctor of Theology

The most difficult, and for many the most important, degree was the doctorate in theology. During the thirteenth and fourteenth centuries the time necessary for the theology doctorate was lengthened rather than shortened. Early in the thirteenth century the course lasted twelve years or more, and the doctor had to be thirty-five years of age. In the reform statutes of

1366,[23] however, we find that the complete course seems to extend over a period of sixteen years, and in 1452 to about fifteen years. In comparison, one might become a master in arts at the age of twenty-one, after some six years of study, and a doctor in law or medicine at about twenty-eight. The long course helps to explain why there were not a large number of theologians who actually possessed the theological doctorate.

The two books used most during this period of study were the Bible and the *Sentences* of Peter Lombard. Those familiar with the Middle Ages are aware that the most-studied book was the Bible.[24] This was true before the universities were formed, and it is not strange to find that the long university course in theology consisted in great part of the study of the Bible.

The medieval universities gave greater place in their schemes of knowledge to theology than do their modern successors. When speaking of the seven liberal arts, Jacques de Vitry, a writer of the first half of the thirteenth century, says:

Logic is good for it teaches us to distinguish true from false; grammar, for it teaches us how to speak and write correctly; rhetoric is good, for it shows us how to speak elegantly and to persuade our hearers; geometry is good by which we learn how to measure the earth, the domain of our bodies; arithmetic teaches us to count the newness of our days; music reminds us of the songs of the blessed in heaven; astronomy makes us think of the celestial

---

[23] Cf. document in Thorndike, *Univ. Records*, pp. 244–247.

[24] The authoritative work of B. Smalley, *The Study of the Bible in the Middle Ages* (Oxford, 1952), begins: "The Bible was the most studied book of the middle ages."

bodies and stars shining brilliantly in God's presence. But theology is better by far than these others. It alone can really be called a liberal art, since it alone liberates the human soul from its troubles.

In the actual study of theology the medieval theologians taught the Bible and the *Sentences* of Peter Lombard by the same educational techniques used in the other faculties. There were the "ordinary" lectures, which were then reviewed and learned more thoroughly by the various types of disputations both inside and outside private classes, as well as "extraordinary" lectures by the bachelors in theology on various books of the Bible or on the *Sentences*. The students and master would have a copy of the text before them, with the students following the text and the master's commentaries as well as the glosses. The *Sentences* of Peter Lombard was probably the most popular manual of theology ever penned, and some idea of it must be had to understand the theology course.

Peter Lombard was born about 1100 in Novara, or perhaps Lumello, in Italy, and lived until 1160 or 1164. He studied at Bologna, at Rheims, and at Paris. At Rheims, St. Bernard provided for him and also presented him with a letter of recommendation addressed to the Abbot of St. Victor. One of his pupils, John of Corwall, tells us that Peter studied the works of Abelard very carefully, and actually studied under him in 1136. We find him again at Rheims with Robert of Melun some years later. In 1159 he was appointed Archbishop of Paris, but he held the office for only a short period, being succeeded by Maurice de Sully, the builder of the cathedral of Notre Dame. Peter wrote this book, which made him famous for centuries, while he was a professor at Notre Dame.

The work itself, divided into four books, discusses by means of a long series of questions and organizes into one body the great mass of theological materials. In the first book, Peter treats of God and the Blessed Trinity, of God's attributes, of His providence, of predestination and of evil. In the second, he writes of creation, the angels and devils, the fall of Adam, the gift of supernatural grace, and of sin; in the third, of the Incarnation, the redemption of man, the virtues and the Ten Commandments; in the fourth, of the sacraments in general, of the seven sacraments in particular, and then of the four last things—that is, of death, judgment, heaven, and hell.

This work of Peter Lombard was an attempted *via media* between the two great tendencies of the twelfth century— the emphasis on reason and speculation, as evidenced in Abelard and his colleagues, and the reliance on authority and the teachings of the early Fathers of the Church, as evidenced by St. Bernard and theologians of like mind. Between these two strong tendencies, Peter steered his middle way, attempting to combine good points of both sides. Making full use of the Bible and the Fathers, he employed the helps that reason afforded in expounding the various points of theological doctrine. Basically, he was a compiler, but the value of his work is incontestable. Some few statements amidst the great mass of doctrinal content were either abandoned or condemned by later theological opinion; but, by and large, Peter Lombard came up with a theological work that was *the* textbook, apart from the Bible, for more than five hundred years. Each candidate for a biblical doctorate had to study it for four years and teach from it for two years more during the long course of his studies.

Other books were consulted and studied by the medieval

theological student besides the Bible and the *Sentences*. For example, there were compilations of questions discussed by the professors, as well as the many *"summae"* written during this period. There were the commentaries on various parts of the Bible, given as lectures by the students in their bachelor days and frequently taken down by a "reporter," who thus produced the *reportatio*, as it was called. Sometimes the lecturer then took these notes and rewrote them before allowing them to circulate under his name. These *summae*, or summaries of the main points and questions discussed, were very lengthy, and the famous *Summa Theologica* of St. Thomas Aquinas is a case in point. This magnificent theological summary, containing hundreds of "questions" and thousands of objections and their answers, covers much the same ground as the materials in the *Sentences*. The preface in this, the greatest of the *summae*, and one which has stimulated and developed so much theological thought during the past seven hundred years, gives the student pause:

The doctor of Catholic truth ought not only to instruct the proficient, but also to teach beginners. As St. Paul says, *As unto little ones in Christ, I gave you milk to drink, not meat* (I Cor. iii, 1–2). For this reason it is our purpose in the present work to treat of the things which belong to the Christian religion in such a way as befits the instruction of beginners.

For we have observed that beginners in this doctrine have been considerably hampered by what various authors have written. They have been hampered partly because of the multiplication of useless questions, articles and arguments; partly, too, they have been hampered because those things that are needful for them to know are not taught according to the order of the subject matter, but rather according as the order of exposition in books demands, or according as the occasion for disputation arises; and partly they have been hampered because frequent repetition brought about weariness and confusion in the minds of the readers.

It will be our endeavor to avoid these and other like faults. With confidence in God's help, we shall try, following the needs of the subject matter, to set forth briefly and clearly the things which pertain to sacred doctrine.[25]

Such, then, were the various textbooks and student-aids used by the different faculties of the medieval universities. Recent research has tended to modify the opinion that medieval students did not have at hand copies of the ordinary materials lectured on; it now seems clear that the students had available such texts and other student-aids besides, such as parts of a *summa*, or compilations of the "questions" so often discussed in the various scholastic exercises. At times they rented a treatise for the length of the course or borrowed a copy from some other student.

It is a striking coincidence that the majority of "great books" for the various faculties were produced, compiled, translated, or commented on during the twelfth century, but it remained for the university organizations of the thirteenth century to take these various works and make them the basic tools for university training.

If the modern university student is treated to a series of textbooks in his various courses, it is to the thirteenth century and the age of the medieval universities that he must look for their origins. In one sense this emphasis of the medieval university teachers upon the same standard works could be called the age of the canonization of the texts.

[25] Quoted from *The Basic Writings of Saint Thomas Aquinas*, edited by Anton C. Pegis (New York: Random House, 1945), I, Prologue.

CLASS HOURS

The medieval student seems to have been a hardier individual than his modern successor when it comes to certain aspects of his ordinary class schedule. At least he started classes a bit earlier than is our wont today. Generally, the first lecture of the daily grind seems to have begun about six in the morning or, at the latest, about seven. There is a daily class schedule which has come down to us from the University of Leipzig, unfortunately a bit later than one would like (1519), but undoubtedly mirroring conditions which were customary. According to this timetable the student began classes at 6 A.M. with a lecture on metaphysics! At Bologna the student attended a lecture in the morning which had to be finished by tierce (9 A.M.), and then two lectures in the afternoon, from 2 to 4 P.M. and from 4 to 5:30 during the winter, or from 1:30 to 3 P.M. and from 3:30 to 5 P.M. during the summer. Robert Goulet in his account of the University of Paris (1517) presents his ideal schedule for a student:

Rise at 4 A.M.
Arts lecture at 5
Mass at 6, breakfast
The regents go to their classes 8–10 (or 9–11 during Lent)
Formal debates before the noon meal
Repetitions
Lectures 3–5
Disputations 5–6
Repetitions after evening meal
Off to bed at 9 P.M.

The average lecture often lasted for two hours. For example, the city regulations of the commune of Bologna

(1475) with regard to the professors whose salary was paid by the city declared that those professors were required to lecture for one or two hours, according to the statutes of the university. At Padua, the doctor or professor was directed by statute to lecture for two hours, and students were forbidden, likewise by statute, to beat upon desks or benches to bring him to an earlier stop!

There were, as we have already noted, two chief types of lectures, one called the "ordinary" lecture and the other called the "extraordinary" at Bologna or the "cursory" at Paris. The difference between these two kinds of instruction has been a disputed point, but it now seems safe to say that they are distinguished by several characteristics. Usually, the "ordinary" lectures were the most important and formed the basis of the curriculum; they were generally given during the morning hours and by the salaried professors. The "extraordinary" lectures were delivered later on in the day, and frequently, especially at Paris, they covered the matter in a more "cursory" way. Sometimes they were given by the bachelors and were presented sketchily by way of review. Thus it might happen that a book was taken in the "ordinary" way one year, and in the following year studied in a briefer—more of a survey—presentation. The student might hear it in this way either for the first time or by way of review.

Besides these formal lectures there were other intellectual exercises from which learning might be gained. First, there were various kinds of disputations. *A disputation basically is the presentation, explanation, and proof of some statement or theory and the answering of objections against it put by an opponent.* Sometimes the defender would be a student in a private class, where for the sake of practice this sort of review might be demanded weekly; at other times the apprentice teacher, the "bachelor"[26] was the defendant and answered objections put to him by another; or again, the defendant might be the professor himself, who held the field against all comers. Young students present at these various kinds of intellectual tournaments naturally learned from others' experiences.

Another type of scholastic exercise was a kind of catechetical repetition of the materials covered in class during which the scholars were quizzed about the lecture either by the lecturer himself or someone else. It is thus described in an ordinance for Louvain in 1476:

... After lunch, each one having brought to the table his books, all the scholars of the Faculty together, in the presence of a tutor, shall review that regular lecture; and in the review the tutor shall follow a method which will enable him by discreet questioning of every man to find out if each of them listened well to the lecture and remembered it and which will also recall the whole lecture by having its parts recited by individuals. And if watchful care is used in this, one hour will suffice.[27]

There were numerous holidays during the scholastic year.[28] In fact at Bologna, if there was no holiday during the week, Thursday was taken as the day off for that week. On these feast days the ordinary and extraordinary lectures were not given, but on other subjects lectures were allowed; for example,

[26] Cf. *infra*, "From Apprentice to Master."
[27] Quoted from A. Norton, *Readings in the History of Education* (Cambridge, 1909), p. 132. These and subsequent citations have been quoted with the permission of Harvard University Press.
[28] Cf. document in Thorndike, *Univ. Records*, pp. 188–189.

in the Rules for the University of Paris[29] as given in 1215 by the cardinal legate Robert de Courçon, it is stipulated that "they shall not lecture on feast days except on philosophers and rhetoric and the *quadrivium* and *Barbarismus* (*Ars Maior* of Donatus, Book III), and ethics if it please them, and the fourth book of the *Topics*." Thus on holidays students could pick up additional knowledge, oftentimes on various subjects of the *trivium* or *quadrivium*.

The history of the student vacations in the Middle Ages is one of expansion! In 1231 Gregory XI, in his reformatory bull "the Magna Carta of Paris University," lays down that "henceforward the summer vacation shall not exceed one month," and he allowed the bachelors to continue their lectures if they wished. At the end of the fourteenth century, however, the long vacation began on the vigil of the feast day of Sts. Peter and Paul (June 28) and lasted until the feast of St. Louis for the faculty of arts (August 25) or until the day after the Exaltation of the Holy Cross (September 16) for the faculties of theology and canon law. At these dates, lectures could be begun, but actually it seems that the feast of St. Remigius (October 1) was the formal opening of the school term. There were two major divisions in the school year; the "great ordinary," from October 1 to Easter, and the "little ordinary," from Easter until the end of June. There were a few days off at Christmas and Easter, and even during the "long vacation" "cursory" lectures could still be given.

The place of lectures is one of the great differences between the medieval university and its modern counterpart. In the be-

[29] Cf. Document 2, Appendix.

111

ginning the professor used his own room or rooms, and when the classes became too large he would have to hire a hall. Later on at Paris, for example, the nations had their own schools for the "ordinary" lectures. For the "extraordinary" type, the teacher had to fend for himself. At Bologna for the large student assemblies, or for doctoral inceptions, they used a nearby church or the cathedral. The master, or professor, paid his own rent to some individual owner of the building. Later on, by 1400, when the various nations at Paris owned their own buildings, the master rented from them instead. If the master did not have a benefice or salary, he was dependent on the fees of his students, chiefly those levied at the "determination" of his bachelors. The college system brought about an advantage to the master because the college furnished him a place to teach and relieved him of any rent problems.

A MEDIEVAL CLASS IN CANON LAW

The following description attempts to give a synopsized example of an imaginary "ordinary" lecture in one of the law faculties. With a change of subject material, the same technique could be transferred to the other faculties. This summary is based on the longer translation of the 37th distinction of Gratian's *Decretum*, in Arthur O. Norton's *Readings in the History of Education*.[30] Although the extract presents only parts of the discussion, it does give some idea of how the class was conducted. The gloss was not at the bottom of the page, but either in between the lines or at the sides of the page, so that the medieval texts had side-notes instead of foot-notes.

[30] Pp. 59–75. Cf. also *infra*, p. 153.

Apart from this, the technique should be familiar enough to the modern student.

In the system followed in these examples, the numbered notes (1, 2, 3) refer to the ordinary gloss and the notes marked with a letter of the alphabet (a, b, c, etc.) are *notes to the gloss.* Thus one can see how the critical apparatus and annotations gradually overshadowed the text. Sometimes the notes are merely summaries to aid the student to understand the text; at other times they are references to the source of the quotation, or to other parts of the *Decretum* where similar materials are treated.

If we imagine ourselves in a rented classroom in Bologna in December, 1280, we might hear something like the following lecture by a doctor of laws seated at his rostrum-type desk, with the students sitting on benches, some following the lecture in their copy of the text while others are taking notes.

The question which we are treating of this morning in Gratian's decretals reads as follows. The question is asked whether priests should read secular literature.[1] The summary of the section says that this is the 37th division, in which the question is asked whether it is fitting that the clergy be made acquainted with the books of the heathen. First, he proves that they should not be read; then he proves the opposite; and finally he gives his solution.

[1] *The gloss* says: In this thirty-seventh division Gratian asks (a) if one who is to be ordained should be acquainted with pagan literature. First, he shows that the clergy should not pay heed to the books of the heathen. (b) Second he gives arguments on the other side and offers this solution, that some read the books of the pagans for amusement and pleasure and this is forbidden, while some read for instruction and this is lawful, in order that by these books they may know how to speak correctly and to tell the true from the false. . . . Notice that in all the citations up to *"but on the other hand"* pleasure alone seems to be forbidden.

Here is what is written upon the matter in the fourth Council of Carthage. A bishop ought not to read pagan literature.[1] A bishop ought not to read the books of the heathen: those of the heretics he may read carefully either by reason of necessity[2] or for some other special reason. Thus Jerome writes to Pope Damasus "on the prodigal son."

Priests are blameworthy who, to the neglect of the Gospels, read the pagan comedies. We see priests of God, who to the neglect of the Gospels and the Prophets are reading comedies, singing the "amatory" words of verses, keeping Vergil in their hands and making of that which boys have to study necessarily,[3] a ground of accusation against themselves because they do it for pleasure. He gives another argument: *They walk in the vanity and darkness of the senses who occupy themselves with secular learning.*[4]

Does he not seem to be walking in vanity . . . who day and night torments himself with the dialectic art; who, as an investigator of nature, lifts his eyes to the heavens . . . who grows enthusiastic over iambics . . . who in his overzealous mind, analyses and com-

---

[1] *The gloss* here says: therefore they ought not to hear the laws for it is a disgrace to them if they wish to be versed in forensic education. But on the other hand the laws are divinely promulgated through the mouths of princes as xvi question, iii, "Nemo" (reference to another part of Gratian). Some declare it is lawful to hear the laws so that by them canon law may be better understood. He argues in favor of this division in the section beginning "Some read profane literature." Comment of John the Teuton.

    a. Incidentally, Comment of Hugo of Pisa.

    b. And Gratian continues this as far as the section starting: "But on the other hand."

[2] In order that they may learn how to speak correctly.

[3] *The gloss* notes: In order that they may know how to speak correctly.

[4] *Summary.* Four classes of men are blamed here, i.e., dialecticians who spend their day wrestling with the dialectic art; the physicists who scan the heavens; versifiers; and the avaricious who obtain wealth without regard to justice even though at the time they do not know to whom they are going to bequeath it.

bines the great jungle of metres; and (to speak of another angle of the matter) who seeks after riches by any means fair or foul, who flatters kings, grasps at the inheritances of others, and accumulates wealth although he does not know at the time to whom he will leave it?

Jerome gives another argument in commenting on a passage of Isaiah for he says; He who misunderstands the Sacred Scriptures or makes a wrong use of secular wisdom is drunken with wine and with strong drink.[1] They are thus drunk with wine who[2] do not understand the Scriptures and pervert them, and, through strong drink, they make a wrong use of secular wisdom and the tricks of the dialecticians which are to be called not so much tricks as figures. That is, they are symbols and images which quickly pass away and are destroyed. Also, in agreement with tropology[3] we should look on men as false prophets who interpret the words of the Scriptures in another way than the Holy Spirit utters them, and as divine those who from the inferences of their own minds

[1] *Summary*. Under this heading, Jerome describes five cases. For he says that those are drunk with wine who misunderstand and pervert the scriptures. Secondly, those who make a wrong use of profane wisdom. Thirdly, he explains who should be called false prophets; fourthly, who are divine, and fifthly he shows that he eats sour grapes who explains the Sacred Scriptures otherwise than according to the truth even though his explanation go not directly against the faith.

[2] The ears of those who misunderstand the words of the Master should be cut off. Cf. 24th question, I *"Si Petrus."* (a)

[3] That is, in accordance with the moral meaning from the word trope, i.e., a turning (b) or application when we apply our words to the formation of character. Cf. XIIII distinction. Beginning, *"Sit Rector."* An addition. They did the opposite and he writes of penitence, cf. distinction 1, beginning *"Super tribus."*

  (a) The ears of those who misunderstand should be torn off. Tropology.

  (b) and the Greek word, logos, speech, whence tropologia that is the (moral) application of the language. Hugo of Pisa. On this matter cf. distinction 76, *"Jejunium"* at end of passage.

115

and apart from the authority of the divine words, proclaim as true the uncertain events of the future. Also, those men can be said to eat sour grapes who do not understand the Scriptures according to the actual truth. (Gratian then gives several more arguments in the form of citations from the Fathers or medieval writers, and then presents arguments on the other side.)

But on the other hand[1] we read that Moses and Daniel were learned in all the wisdom of the Egyptians and Chaldeans. We read also that God ordered the sons of Israel to despoil the Egyptians[2] of their gold and silver; the moral understanding of this teaches us to find in the poets either the gold of wisdom or the silver of eloquence, and that we should turn it to the profit of useful learning. In the book of Leviticus we are commanded to offer to God the first fruits of Honey, that is to say, the sweetness of human eloquence. The Magi also, presented three gifts by which some writers would have us understand the three parts[3] of philosophy.

And for this reason Bede says in the Book of Kings: The clergy should not be prevented from reading secular literature.[4]

He injures the mental acumen of his readers and causes it to grow dim who believes that they should in every way be prevented

[1] *Summary.* From this passage on, Gratian shows that the clergy should be learned in secular literature and knowledge. He uses six considerations to show it. The first is stated at the beginning. The second begins: "We read also." The third begins: "In the book of Leviticus"; the fourth, "The Magi also," and the fifth, "Finally Cassiodorus"; and the sixth, "Therefore Ambrose also. . . ."

[2] Cf. distinction 14, question 5 which begins, "*Dixit.*"

[3] That is to say: ethics, natural philosophy and rational philosophy.

[4] *Summary.* Certain men had forbidden Christians to read the books of the Gentiles, but Bede blames them for this and says that these books can well be read without sin because profit may be derived from them as in the case of Moses and Daniel and also of Paul who incorporated in his Epistles verses of the poets, e.g. "the Cretans. . . ."

from reading secular books; for whatever useful things,[1] are found in them it is lawful to adopt as one's own. If not, then Moses and Daniel would not have been permitted to become learned in the wisdom and literature of the Egyptians and Chaldeans, whose superstitions and immorality they shuddered at. And the teacher[2] of the Gentiles himself would not have introduced some verses of the poets into his own writings or sayings.

Gratian remarks then:

Why[3] are those works forbidden to be read which it is shown so reasonably should be read? Some[4] read secular literature for their pleasure and are delighted with the productions of the poets and the charm of their words; others read them to add to their knowledge so that, through noting the errors of the pagans, they may denounce them, and that they may turn to the service of sa-

[1] For we read that when Paul had reached Athens he saw an altar of the Unknown God on which there was an inscription: "This is an altar of the unknown God in whom we live and move and have our being." And with this inscription the Apostle began his sermon and made known to those Athenians the meaning of this inscription . . . continuing about our God and declaring "Whom you worship in ignorance, that I proclaim to you." Then Dionysius, the Areopagite, seeing a blind man passing by, said to Paul, "If you give sight to that blind man, I will believe you." Immediately, when the name of Christ had been invoked, his sight was restored and Dionysius believed.

[2] For example, in the Epistle of Paul to Titus there is the quotation from Epimenides the poet: cf. Distinction I, question 1, beginning *"Dominus declaravit."* Also in the first Epistle to the Corinthians he introduces a quotation from Menander. I question 1, beginning *"Saepe"* . . . Jerome in his fifth section *on Consecration* often quoted verses from Vergil and Augustine. . . . As a lawyer he uses the authority of Vergil . . . and also of Homer. . . .

[3] *Summary.* Gratian solves the contradiction by pointing out that one should learn secular knowledge in addition, not just for pleasure, but for instruction in order that the useful things found in it, can be turned to the use of sacred learning. So it was that Gregory blamed a certain bishop, not because he acquired profane knowledge but because for his pleasure, he taught grammar instead of the Gospel.

[4] Cf. St. Gregory in his 86th division and in other places.

cred and devout learning the useful material they find there. These are to be praised for adding to their learning the secular literature. For this reason, Gregory of blessed memory did not blame a certain bishop for learning secular literature but he blamed him because, contrary to his obligation as a bishop, he read grammar to the people instead of reading the Gospel lesson.[1] *Therefore Ambrose writes concerning Luke: Profane writings should be read that they may not be unknown.*

Some we read[2] that we may not neglect them;[3] others we read that we may not be ignorant of them; others we read not that we may embrace them but that we may reject them.[4]

Jerome when commenting on the letter to Titus says: *Grammar should be read to help understand the Scriptures.*

If anyone[5] has mastered grammar or dialectics in order to be able to speak correctly and to discriminate between the true and the false, we do not blame them. Geometry[6] and Arithmetic and

[1] (It is interesting to note here how Gratian understands this citation, which sometimes has been cited, as if Gregory were condemning the study of secular literature in general.)

[2] *Summary*. It was reported to Eugene at his Synod that in some places there were no teachers to instruct others in the liberal arts and so he enjoined it on all the bishops to establish teachers in suitable localities to teach others daily in liberal doctrines.

[3] For though they be not of use, yet it is necessary to know them. Cf. Distinction 7, last chapter.

[4] As for example the books of the heretics. Cf. Distinction 24, question 3, last chapter.

[5] *Summary*. This section is divided into two parts. First, it is noted that it is not wrong to learn grammar and logic to distinguish between the true and the false. In the second part (which begins with "Geometry and Arithmetic"), it is noted that the knowledges of the quadrivium have a truth of their own. But they are not the knowledges of piety, and are not to be so applied. The Old and New Testament are knowledges of piety and are to be applied. Grammar, then, if applied to good uses may be made profitable.

[6] Geometry. He does not mention astronomy because this subject has fallen into disuse. Cf. 24, question 2, "*His ita.*"

Music contain truth in their own range of knowledge, but that knowledge is not the knowledge of piety. The knowledge of piety means to know the Law, to understand the Prophets, to believe the Gospel and not to be ignorant of the Apostles. Besides the teaching of the grammarians can contribute to life, provided it has been applied to its higher uses.

(Then Gratian continues the discussion with several citations from various other sources; for instance, canonical collections of papal and synodal materials, as this example shows.)

So too, from the Synod of Pope Eugene: Bishops should appoint teachers and instructors in suitable places.

The report has come to us regarding certain regions that they have neither teachers nor care for the pursuit of letters. Therefore, in every way, care and diligence should be used by all the bishops among the peoples subject to them and in other places where the necessity may arise, that teachers and instructors be appointed to teach zealously the pursuit of letters and the principles of the liberal arts, because in them especially are the divine commands revealed and declared.[1]

(Then, summing up the matter, Gratian draws his own conclusion.)

Therefore, as is evident from the authorities cited, ignorance ought to be hateful to priests. For if in ignorance of their own blindness, they start out to lead others, both of them fall into the ditch. . . . For when those who go ahead are darkened, the ones who follow are easily inclined to bear the burdens of sinners. Therefore, priests must strive to cast off ignorance as if it were a kind of pestilence. . . . (And he ends quoting Augustine.)

Hence Augustine in his book of Questions: Not every man who

---

[1] *Summary.* It was reported to Eugene at his Synod that in some places there were no teachers to instruct others in the liberal arts and so he enjoined it on all the bishops to establish teachers in suitable localities to teach others daily in liberal doctrines.

is ignorant is free from the penalty. For the ignorant person who is ignorant because he found no way of learning (the law) can be excused from the penalty, but he cannot be pardoned who having the means of knowledge did not use them.

The foregoing example would be something like a medieval class lecture from the decretals. The method of glossing or quoting various commentators on the text and writing that commentary in the text, either between the lines (interlinear commentaries) or out at the edge of the page (marginal commentaries), was used in the other faculties as well. The reader will have noted the constant reference to original sources and the practical knowledge of the relevant passages. He will also have noted how the commentaries were becoming a heavy mass of materials, often overshadowing the text. On the other hand, this use of primary sources in argumentation is a technique of perennial value.

ADDITIONAL READINGS

Castiglioni, A., *A History of Medicine,* trans. by E. B. Krumbhaar (New York, 1947).
Cicognani, A. G., *Canon Law* (Philadelphia, 1934), especially pp. 265–289.
Garrison, F. H., *Introduction to the History of Medicine,* 4th ed. (Philadelphia, 1929).
Ghellinck, Joseph de, "The Liber Sententiarum," *Dublin Review,* CXLVI (1910), 139–166.
Le Bras, "Gratian," *Encyclopedia of Social Sciences,* VII.
———, "Canon Law," *The Legacy of the Middle Ages,* edited by C. G. Crump and E. F. Jacob (Oxford, 1932).

Gilson, Etienne, *History of Christian Philosophy in the Middle Ages* (New York, 1955).

Gordon, Benjamin, *Medieval and Renaissance Medicine* (New York, 1959).

Kibre, P., "Hippocratic Writings in the Middle Ages," *Bulletin of the History of Medicine*, XVIII (1945), 371–412.

——, "The Faculty of Medicine at Paris, Charlatanism, and Unlicensed Medical Practices in the Later Middle Ages," *Bulletin of the History of Medicine*, XXVII (1953), 1–20.

MacKinney, L. C., "Medical Education in the Middle Ages," *Journal of World History*, II, No. 4 (1955).

Meynial, Ed., "Roman Law," *The Legacy of the Middle Ages.*

Norton, A., *Readings in the History of Education: Medieval Universities* (Cambridge, Mass., 1909).

Paetow, L. J., *The Arts Course at Medieval Universities with Special Reference to Grammar and Rhetoric*, University of Illinois, The University Studies, III, No. 7 (Urban, Ill., 1910).

Rashdall, H., Powicke, F.M., Emden, A.B., *The Universities of Europe in the Middle Ages* (Oxford, 1936), 3 vols.

Smalley, B., *The Study of the Bible in the Middle Ages* (Oxford, 1952).

Thorndike, L., *University Records and Life in the Middle Ages*, University of Columbia, Records of Civilization, XXXVIII (New York, 1944).

Walsh, James J., *Medieval Medicine* (London, 1920).

——, *Old Time Makers of Medicine* (New York, 1911).

IV. FROM APPRENTICE TO MASTER IN SIX TO SIXTEEN YEARS

The medieval university took the young student as an apprentice to learning, placed him under the guidance of those who had mastered the intellectual skills, and trained him for several years in this fashion. Then, when a certain point in his intellectual formation had been reached, the young student was turned into a young professor (somewhat like a teaching-fellow) while continuing with his graduate studies. The relationship of knowledge and teaching was a close one in the medieval university concept of a scholar; hence, the tendency to bring about a closer relation between graduate study and teaching has good medieval precedent. Although many of the university doctors or masters of arts did not teach, the medieval university operated as a teacher-training system, and a degree meant a permission to begin to teach.

The medieval approach to the problem was simple. They believed that the way to teach a student philosophy, for example, was to place him under the care and teaching supervision of a master of that subject. By this means the student would learn philosophy. They thought that those who conducted the organization where things were taught should themselves be teachers. Thus the rector in the medieval university, the proctors in the nations, were *teachers elected by a*

122

body of teachers from a body of teachers to supervise a place where teaching was going on.

Recalling the guild training of an apprentice to become a journeyman and then a master-workman, we can see the similarity in the progress of the medieval university student from his inception as an intellectual apprentice until his "commencement" as a university master or doctor.

The Prerequisites for the University Student

The first thing that the medieval university freshman really *had* to have to go to class was a knowledge of Latin. All lectures and all texts used that language. So before the student could profit from instruction, he had to be able to read, write, and understand such Latin as was used in the schools. Then too, the student body came from various parts of Europe and spoke many dialects, so that the knowledge of some Latin as a common language was a necessity. Later on, when colleges and halls became common, their statutes required the students to use Latin. Apparently at that time Latin was pronounced in the same way by both the English and the Continental scholars, so that national vowel pronunciation of Latin was no obstacle. Some students resident at Paris never learned French; for example, Pope John XXII (1316–1334), who studied both at Paris and Orleans, did not learn the French of the Ile-de-France, and when King Charles of France sent a letter in that language in 1323 it had to be translated into Latin. How proficient the student had to be in Cicero's language is difficult to judge. One chantry provision directs that the scholar was to be sent on to

123

the university when he was able to "read, sing and construe well and also compose twenty-four verses on one subject in one day" in Latin.

Medieval Latin was a living language and changed with the changing times. There were, however, different degrees of knowledge and practice of Latin among different types of educated men. The Latinity of a bachelor lecturing on the *Sentences* was definitely not the Latinity of a John of Salisbury in his *Metalogicon*.

Where did the young freshman get his knowledge of Latin, such as it was? First of all, grammar often formed one of the subjects of examination for the degree in arts. Although the arts curriculum was heavily weighted in favor of philosophy, even at Paris the younger arts students attended a certain amount of grammar instruction. In many university towns, and in other cities besides, there were schools for the instruction of young boys in Latin grammar and literature which were distinct from the university. But sometimes the universities, especially in Germany, controlled these schools as well as those proper to the university. At times there was a master of grammar who was regarded as a kind of second-rate member of the arts faculty. At Oxford, in the fourteenth century, the grammar masters were supervised by two masters from the university, and the grammarians had to attend weekly disputations in matters grammatical, just as the philosophy faculty did with regard to philosophy disputations; and in the sixteenth century, Oxford had both a bachelorship and mastership in grammar with the attendant ceremonies of inception. The new master of grammar at his inception did not receive a book as the symbol of his work, as did the other masters, but a "birch rod," and he began by flogging a boy in the schools! We are told that he paid the beadle a groat for the birch rod and gave another groat to the boy "for his labour."

Besides these schools for grammar in the university cities, there were grammar schools in towns and cities not possessing universities. The average student coming from outside the university cities had learned "to read and write and construe" in Latin before he came to the university, very likely at one of the older ecclesiastical schools in connection with parish or cathedral. These cathedral schools taught not only grammar and logic but probably in some cases a full university arts course. The lower clergy in various countries were trained in such schools, and some of these schools later developed into universities. In places where there was no cathedral, the grammar school was attached to the parish, or perhaps to some collegiate church. The most ordinary schoolmaster was the chantry priest or, in his absence, the local parish priest. In the later Middle Ages, the smallest towns and larger villages all had someone about the place who could teach the essentials of ecclesiastical Latin, and many besides the clerics knew some Latin, for the bailiff of the manor kept his records in Latin, and many richer nobles kept a "grammar master" as part of their establishment.

ARTIST AND BACHELOR

Since the degree of master of arts, or at least several years of study in arts, was a prerequisite for the other faculties, the collegian began with arts. When the young grammarian came up to the university, he enrolled in the nation of his district

125

and began his course of studies. How old was the average "freshman" in arts in the medieval university? This question is not easy to answer. It has generally been said that the boys coming up were on the average about fourteen years old, but owing to one document which has "12" instead of what probably should have been "21," the problem has been complicated. The tendency now seems to place the normal freshman age at about fifteen or sixteen. Perhaps it would be fairly accurate to say that the average first-year medieval arts student was about the age of a sophomore or a junior in our high schools.

This period of study of the *artist*—that is to say, before he became a bachelor who had "determined," and was continuing for the licentiate—was divided into two periods. During the first, which usually lasted from four to five years, the apprentice was a student pure and simple who went to class and heard his lectures. He also participated in the class disputations of the teacher and attended various types of disputations.

THE DETERMINATION

The "determination" itself was a series of disputations given at least once a week during Lent under the supervision of the master. After the artist had satisfied the regent master under whom he had worked that he was prepared to go on to his determination, then the next step was the "qualifying" examination, as we might call it, for the actual determination. On this point we have a document for the English-German nation at the University of Paris in 1252 which gives specific directions.[1] It was the nation which supervised this preliminary

[1] Cf. Document 5, Appendix.

examination and passed on the fitness of the candidate to apply for permission to determine, because each nation was interested in seeing that the candidates who would dispute from its ranks would not disgrace it.

The "responsion" at which the bachelor responded to a master seems to have been held in the December previous to the Lent during which the candidate determined. Then followed an examination by certain masters of the nation, whose twofold duty was to ascertain that the student had read the required books and attended the lectures and to test him on what he had learned. The student had to affirm under oath that he had attended the lectures in arts for five, or at least four, years at Paris or at some other *studium generale,* that he had his own master under whom he would determine, and that he would use the schools of a regent master.

The subject matter which the student must have covered was carefully specified in a document for the English nation. The section of Aristotelian works called the "Old Logic" (*On the Predicaments and Interpretation* with sometimes the inclusion also of the *Divisions* and the *Topics*), was to be gone through twice from "ordinary" lectures and once cursorily; the *Six Principles* of Gilbert de la Porrée was to be had once ordinarily and once cursorily; the first three books of the *Topics* and *Divisions* of Boethius, also once cursorily and twice ordinarily; the *Topics* at least twice ordinarily, if not twice ordinarily and once cursorily; the *Sophistical Refutations,* the same number of classes as for the *Topics;* the *Prior Analytics,* once ordinarily and once cursorily; the *Posterior Analytics,* once by ordinary lectures; the *De Anima,* once; the *Two Priscians,* once cursorily; and the *Barbarismus* of Donatus, twice ordinarily and once cursorily. Besides having

127

attended these lectures, the candidate had to affirm on oath that he had attended faithfully the disputations of his teachers for a period of two years.

If a young artist came up for the determination who had not completely complied with all the requirements, the examiners might deal with his special case as they thought best. In 1403 there were some scholars who had not finished the prescribed number of lectures on the *Topics* and some others who had not thus completed the *Prior Analytics*, and they asked to be admitted for the license to teach. In response the nation granted the request only on condition that the students complete the requirements as soon as possible, as the nation did not wish to establish a precedent.

The actual examiners of those coming up for their determination were chosen indirectly in the following fashion. First, the proctor of the nation selected two persons who in his opinion could be relied on to pick good examiners; then these two selected three examiners whom they considered impartial, and these chosen ones must swear that they would allow to proceed to their determination only those who really were prepared and worthy; they had also to promise to act impartially and not be moved by prejudice or favor toward any of the candidates. The masters also had to swear that they would not exert pressure on any examiner to favor certain candidates. Lastly there was another oath binding both master and candidate not to appeal to the nation or university if the decision of the examining committee did not please them.

In the reform of the French nation (January, 1452), allegations of laxity were made in regard to this particular examination. The examiners were said to be mere youths and inexperienced masters, and it was alleged that masters from the province of Paris sometimes monopolized the nation's seal, with sad results. At any rate, in the reform of Cardinal d'Estouteville (1452), one of the regulations required examiners for determination to be masters of at least three years' standing. Apparently some candidates whose intellectual prowess was below the accepted standard occasionally had recourse to the physical, for the applicant at the University of Caen for some examinations had to swear that he would not procure any "damage" to an examiner through himself or through another if matters did not go as he desired. By and large, the examinations were certainly not mere forms, and generally university regents tried to see that fairness was shown to all candidates. Sometimes, however, the sons of the nobility received favor; for example, at Toulouse the chancellor could dispense from public examination those who maintained companions in livery, and Cambridge dispensed from the "general" examination and a year's residence the sons of English nobility even as late as the year 1884.

The artist had to secure his permission to determine by the Sunday before Lent (*Quinquagesima*) at the latest, and then he could study and lecture all through Lent; if he could not perform that Lent, he could get a deferment to a subsequent penitential season. He had to swear that he would begin his disputations before the Wednesday after the first week of Lent and continue them throughout Lent, or at least until the middle of Lent in the event that he used a sub-determiner. The student determined under his master, paying him for the use of his classroom; this fee was one of the main hopes of the master for getting back his yearly rent or some large

129

portion of it. At Oxford, however, the master was not allowed to receive anything from the determiner *"pro pensione scholarum."*

During the time of determination the master supervised the work of his young determinant. This seems to have been strongly insisted on, to judge from an appeal, at a congregation meeting of the English nation on March 9, 1371, of one Alexander Fabri de Tharbato, who apparently began his determination before Lent under a master who did not continue his supervision. The nation decided that the master's neglect should not harm the determiner, who was allowed to continue. After he finished his determination the artist could lay claim to the word "bachelor" in its strict technical sense. Incidentally, the word bachelor (Latin: *baccalaureus*) has had a hard go of it with the dictionaries. One derivation is equivalent to the word "cowboy"! The word means, in a general way, a beginner, and in its technical university use it apparently means a student who has finished his determination and is now entering upon another stage of his academic career.

If a determinant did not want to determine throughout his period (something like once a week or so during the whole of Lent), he could sometimes arrange to have a sub-determiner. The sub-determiner, seemingly, carried on from about the middle of Lent, and had to take the same oaths and make the same promises, practically, as the determiner, but he *did not have to pay a burse*, and he did not have to determine throughout the six weeks. Detailed documentation about the system of sub-determiners is lacking, but we know that in 1275 the substitution of a sub-determiner received the sanction and approval of the faculty of arts, that the primary requisite for a sub-determiner was his poverty, and that he was excused from paying the burse necessarily paid by every determiner. The applicant had to establish that he could not pay the required fees, and this was judged by the amount that he paid for his weekly board and room. The proctor of the nation made the inspection, and the permission to sub-determine was granted by the proctor and sanctioned by the consent of the masters given in congregation.

After 1252 there seems to have been a tendency to shorten the arts degree. One regulation required that the determiner be at least fourteen years of age, but this number would seem to be a copyist's mistake; if not, it certainly shows a great difference from the 1252 statute with its minimum age of twenty years. Furthermore, in later decades, the determinant swore that he had heard lectures for at least two years, although the subject matter was the same as previously. There is evidently some difficulty here as regards the number of times that students were to have attended lectures on the various books of Aristotle, if the number was as was required in 1252—or else they had a very heavy class schedule for two years! In addition, the determiner took his oath of obedience to the rector and the proctor and promised to attend the Mass and vespers held during Lent and on special feast days by the nation. He also had to swear that he would give full support to the prosecution of anyone who injured a regent master.

During the period when the new bachelor was determining and defending his various theses, as large as possible an attendance at his performance was desirable. If he or his friends could not persuade others by logic and eloquence to attend, they sometimes pulled in passersby by force or raided the audience of some popular determiner! There was a certain amount of wine provided at the determiner's expense, and at the end of the period of determination there was a feast, a smaller imitation of the master's inception banquet.

When the determiner had finished his determination and joined the ranks of full-fledged bachelors of arts, he would then decide whether to proceed with his education or not. Many stopped as bachelors of arts, since they could obtain positions as teachers in some of the smaller schools in other parts of Europe where bachelors from Paris were in demand. For example, we read of the application of one teacher for a letter of recommendation and a testimonial that he was a bachelor of arts and possessed of a sufficiency of learning, since he wished to return to his native country and teach in the schools of that region.

ON TO THE DOCTORATE

If the bachelor decided to continue for his master's in arts, then he had further years of study, lecture, and disputation ahead of him. The decree of 1366[2] lists the various works to be studied not as a whole group, but as they were taken by the student in his progress toward a master's degree. After his bachelorship, and before he petitioned for his license to teach, the student must have "heard at Paris or in another university" the following Aristotelian works: *Physics, On Generation and Corruption, On the Heavens,* and the *Parva Naturalia;* namely, the treatises of Aristotle *On Sense and Sensation, On Waking and Sleeping, On Memory and Remembering, On the Length*

[2] Cf. document in Thorndike, *Univ. Records*, pp. 244–247.

132

and Shortness of Life. He must also have heard (or have plans to hear) *On the Metaphysics,* and have attended lectures on the mathematical books. Rashdall, when speaking of the Oxford curriculum, gives the following list of works,[3] to be read by the bachelor between the period of his determination and his inception (mastership): books on the liberal arts: in grammar, Priscian; in rhetoric, Aristotle's *Rhetoric* (three terms), or the *Topics* of Boethius (bk. iv), or Cicero's *Nova Rhetorica* or Ovid's *Metamorphoses* or *Poetria Virgilii;* in logic, Aristotle's *De Interpretatione* (three terms) or Boethius *Topics* (bks. 1–3) or the *Prior Analytics* or *Topics* (Aristotle); in arithmetic and in music, Boethius; in geometry, Euclid, Alhacen, or Vitellio, *Perspectiva;* in astronomy, *Theorica Planetarum* (two terms), or Ptolemy, *Almagesta.* In natural philosophy the additional works are: the *Physics* or *On the Heavens* (three terms) or *On the Properties of the Elements* or the *Meteorics* or *On Vegetables and Plants* or *On the Soul* or *On Animals* or any of the *Parva naturalia;* in moral philosophy, the *Ethics* or *Economics* or *Politics* of Aristotle for three terms; and in metaphysics, the *Metaphysics* for two terms or for three terms if the candidate had not determined.

Between the bachelorship and the mastership, the student must secure his licentiate, which was a permission to teach granted by the ecclesiastical authorities. There were two places in Paris where this could be obtained, either from the bishop's chancellor at Notre Dame or the abbot's chancellor at Ste. Geneviève du Mont. The examiners for this examination were also selected by the nation, and in 1259 Alexander IV decreed

---

[3] Although, as the editors of the more recent edition note, he is compiling from materials later than the thirteenth century.

133

that there should be four examiners for this, one selected from each of the four nations. The English-German nation at Paris usually selected their examiners for both the determination and the licentiate at the same congregation. Usually three or four auditions were sufficient for the number of candidates who presented themselves, and the examinations could be taken at Notre Dame or Ste. Geneviève du Mont. There were no definite rules to direct the candidate to one rather than the other. The licenses do not usually state where they were granted. Although there is a remark in the documents of the English-German nation at Paris that Ste. Geneviève is "the Examination of the faculty of arts," this remark is made about the year 1448. Again in 1470 the proctor of this nation declares that the nation wishes its scholars to be warned by its masters that they are to take their examination at Ste. Geneviève. During the Great Western Schism (1378-1417) the English-German nation, which favored the Roman line (as did England), would not recognize the competency of Notre Dame to grant the license to teach. In 1382–1383 its scholars were forbidden to take their examination there; should they dare to do so, the proctor was not to receive their burses nor allow them to incept under the masters of his nation.

The composition and number of the examining board for the licentiate varied somewhat during the centuries, and it is difficult to make general statements in regard to these examinations. At any rate, the candidate was examined on additional books and had to swear to another batch of propositions. For instance, a student about to come up for his license in the English-German nation came before the nation and swore obedience to the rector and proctor and promised to serve the

134

nation as well as he could. He promised to obey the statutes of the arts faculty and the English nation, and that before beginning his lectures he would pay the five required burses to the receptor of the English nation and would not forget his beadle. Then, before the assembled nations of the faculty of arts, he swore that he would not offer or accept bribes, nor give money to the examiner except to pay for the bit of straw on which he sat during the examination; and that he had chosen his master freely without any pecuniary arrangement determining his choice. The candidate also promised that if he later incepted in the faculty of arts, he would teach for two years and dispute for forty days unless he received a special dispensation. He promised that he would give honest information if, as a teacher, he was asked about the qualifications of the bachelors coming up for examination, and that he would keep the regulations about the amount of money to be spent at his inception. He also affirmed that he was not married or a member of a religious order and promised that he would strive to keep the peace between the artists and the theologians, and the regular and secular clergy.

When all these formalities had been gone through, the examinations successfully passed and the battery of oaths taken, then the actual bestowal of the license followed. At Ste. Geneviève, the candidate came forward and knelt in front of the vice-chancellor, who licensed him in the following words:

I, by the authority invested in me by the apostles Peter and Paul, give you the license for lecturing, reading, disputing, and determining and for exercising other scholastic and magisterial acts both in the faculty of arts at Paris and elsewhere, in the name of the Father and of the Son and of the Holy Ghost, Amen.

135

Although the candidate had achieved his permission to go forth and give out the knowledge that he had been accumulating for many years, he was not yet a full-fledged master or doctor. Between the licentiate and the mastership or doctorate lay the ceremonies of inception. In the decree of 1366[4] there was a distinction made between the books for the licentiate and the master in arts, and this decree notes that "no one shall be admitted to the degree of master of arts unless he has heard the said books (previous books listed for B.A. and licentiate) and also the moral works, especially most of the *Ethics* and the *Meteorology*, the first three books at least, all dispensations being forbidden." The exact amount of time between the licentiate and master of arts cannot be determined; it probably varied from six months to three years, and there is one example, at least, of a candidate who received the licentiate and incepted as master in arts on the same day. Very likely it depended on whether the candidate had already "heard" the required books, and whether he was financially able to pay for the required banquet.

THE INCEPTION

The inception as master in arts consisted of several different acts and ceremonies. First, the inceptor appeared before his nation to make more promises: that he would keep high the standards of the nation and not allow a bachelor to determine except in accordance with the customs of the nation and faculty of arts; that he would contribute his share to defraying the cost of the candles given by the nation for use at Notre Dame; that he would be present at Masses and funerals and congre-

4 Cf. document in Thorndike, *Univ. Records*, pp. 244–247.

gations special to the nation; and that he would not reveal the secrets of the nation.[5] Furthermore, he promised that he would give three burses; one to the university, one to the nation, and one to the beadles. Having been accepted by his nation and having sworn the various oaths, he then took part in a solemn series of disputations, the first on the evening before his inception, known—like the Church prayers at that hour—as "vespers," and another on the day of his inception. At his formal inaugural disputation, after receiving his magisterial biretta, a book from the presiding regent, and the kiss of fellowship, he took his seat upon the magisterial chair. After the more intellectual part of the inception ceremonies, the new doctor gave a banquet to the masters and others.

With these ceremonies the candidate reached the doctorate or mastership in arts. He had received his master's biretta, and now at his ordinary lectures he could wear the round cape and shoes which, at least according to the statutes, were not to be pointed or embroidered.

Of all those incepting in arts, many continued to teach in the arts college; others went to distant colleges or universities to teach. Some for whom the degree was the terminal point in their academic life sought preferment in ecclesiastical or civil service. Others continued their studies in another faculty—that of law, medicine, or theology.

THE YOUNG DOCTOR OF MEDICINE

There was a close connection between the arts course and that of medicine in the medieval university, but the required number of "pre-medic" years in arts is not clear. The student

[5] Cf. document in Thorndike, *Univ. Records*, pp. 103–105.

became a bachelor of medicine and proceeded toward a licentiate or doctorate in medicine as did the arts bachelor. Thus he had to study a certain number of books, attend a certain number of lectures, give some courses in a "cursory" way himself, and take part in a certain number of important disputations. At Bologna, for example, the student, in order to make the step from bachelor of medicine to the doctorate, had to be twenty years of age, to have had five years in the study of medicine, and to be "sufficient in arts." If he had the licentiate in arts, then he needed only four years in medicine. He had to have lectured on some medical book and to have responded or disputed at least twice in the schools. The period required for the licentiate in arts in Italy was somewhat briefer than in Paris; it seems to have taken only four instead of six or seven years, and this seems also to have been the case in some of the German universities. There is a document for Paris (about 1270–1274) which throws light on the practice and requirements there. Bachelors at Paris wishing to start a course had to establish that they had attended lectures in medicine for three years and were in their fourth year, of which they had already put in five months of classroom attendance. Even if he had not spent a full nine months each year in medical study, the applicant could still get permission to teach if he had studied medicine carefully at Paris for thirty-two months; that is, in ordinary lectures without counting the time of vacations. The candidate had to swear further that he had responded twice in the classes of two masters at a formal disputation, or once at a general one; that the text on which he petitioned to lecture cursorily, he had heard ordinarily; that he would attend Mass, as did the masters. He also promised to give the four burses that every bachelor gave who offered a new course.

When the bachelor of medicine came up for his licentiate at Paris, he had to be recommended by his master, and to establish that he had attended lectures for five and a half years if he was a licentiate in arts and six if not. There were other promises to be given as to the number of books heard in ordinary courses, and so on. At Oxford, the period for a M.A. in medicine was some six years. For admission at Oxford to the *"ad practicandum"* privilege, the candidates who were masters in arts needed four years of study; for those who were not, it seems to have taken eight years.

At Montpellier's famous school of medicine in 1340 the length of time for the bachelorship in medicine was fixed at twenty-four months of actual lecture attendance. There the ordinary lectures were over by Easter-time, and the custom was for the bachelors and senior students to spend their summers ·in practice, frequently away from Montpellier. It was also necessary for the young student before he became a bachelor to make a round of visits with his own doctor. For those who had their masters of arts, the course in medicine lasted some five years; for those without it, about six. A statute of 1309 allowed a college student about nine years for the whole course. There was a decree of 1239 which stated that no scholar, under pain of excommunication, could assume his independent practice unless he had been examined and had obtained letters of authorization from both his examiners and the bishop.

Thus the young student of medicine followed the same general pattern of studying, hearing lectures, disputing and responding as was followed in the arts course. When he had "heard" the required books, attended the disputations, fulfilled his requirements in these matters and those of a bachelor lecturer, he could come up for his licentiate and doctorate in medicine. He would "incept" as others incepted in the arts; sometimes, in addition to the other insignia at his graduation ceremonies, the new doctor of medicine was girded with a golden cincture.

THE MEDIEVAL LAWYER

Those studying for a degree in either canon or civil law went through a similar type of lecture and disputation training, using the technique of logical analysis and synthesis, defense and argument, thesis and disputation, on the great collections of Gratian's *Decretals* or the various parts of Justinian's codes. After some five years of study, a student of civil law could begin to lecture on a single "title" of the civil code or, after six years, on a whole book. Permission to begin to lecture on a title in law was granted at Bologna by the rector, at other places by an individual doctor or by the chancellor. The bachelor in law could lecture twice a week, and those permitted to lecture on a whole book might give a repetition. Before taking his doctorate the bachelor had to complete eight years in civil law, which in a statute of 1432 was qualified to "at least seven years"; the doctor in canon law had to finish six years. One could, however, study both canon and civil law together, and it was possible to finish the double doctorate (the famous J.U.D., *Doctor utriusque Juris*) in ten years, according to the statutes of 1432.

140

The doctoral candidate in law had an examination by qualified doctors as in the arts. The important examination was the
"private" one, while that which followed, though public, was
more or less of a formality, and somewhat resembled the "inception" in the mastership of arts. Before presenting him for the
examination, the teacher ascertained for himself the fitness of
his candidate to try the intellectual hurdles. At Bologna before
the admission to either the "private" or the "public" examination the applicant was presented by the *consilarius* of his nation to the rector of the university for the permission, and the
candidate then swore that he had complied with all the various
conditions, that he would give no more than the regulation
fees and banquets to the rector, the doctor, or fellow students,
and that he would obey the rector.

Within eight days before the private examination, the bachelor was presented by his own doctor or another to the archdeacon. After the Mass of the Holy Ghost on the day of examination, the bachelor came before the assembled college of doctors, and one of them assigned him two passages in either civil
or canon law. He then went home to "bone up" as quickly as
he could on all possible ramifications of these passages. Later
in the day the group of examiners reassembled with the archdeacon presiding and listened to an exposition of the selected
passages, after which they proposed questions and difficulties.
The candidate was examined with special care by two doctors,
appointed by the college for the task, but then other lawyers
could ask additional questions after affirming on oath that they
had not communicated these to the candidate. The questions
were on the matter at hand, or relevant materials. In 1387 a
statute decreed that all the doctors of law in turn had to argue

with the candidate. At Cologne the candidate was permitted eight hours to study on the "points" assigned and gave his lecture in the evening of that day.

When the examination was over, the doctors balloted and the archdeacon announced the results. The place of examination was often a public building or the cathedral for the private examination, but in the later fourteenth century the bishop's palace or the doctor's house was used. The public examination was held in the cathedral.

With the first examination finished, the candidate at Bologna was licensed, in the sense that he could proceed with the ceremonies which would make him a fully accepted doctor. Sometimes he proceeded immediately through the remaining ceremonies; sometimes, because of the expense involved, he postponed them for a time. He might even go off to a smaller university where the cost of the ceremony would be less because of a smaller faculty to be presented with individual "gifts." For example, Bologna allowed the candidate to take his doctorate at Padua, where the ceremony was less expensive (but later on, when Padua became famous, the charges there were higher). Ferrara, with a small law faculty, was cheaper than either of them.

Before the actual day of the public ceremonies, the candidate rode about the city preceded by university officials, the beadles of the archdeacon among them, to invite public officials and friends to the grand ceremony. During this trip the statutes forbade the blowing of trumpets, and the like, but on the day of the ceremony itself there was no such prohibition. On this day the candidate, accompanied by a retinue of his

142

fellow students and the presenting doctor, "incepted," in the term used in the northern universities, by actually lecturing and disputing. This was similar to the procedure in Roman law whereby one was invested with his office by an actual performance of its functions. At this ceremony, the candidate was also admitted into the guild of doctors, although at Bologna by the end of the thirteenth century such admission did not carry full privileges of actually teaching there.[6]

When he had arrived at the place of the *conventus*, or public examination, the candidate gave a speech and then read a thesis on some point of law which he defended against opponents chosen from among the student body, thus acting as a doctor in a university disputation. When this was finished, he was again presented to the archdeacon by his "promoter" (his presenting doctor). The archdeacon then gave a short talk praising the candidate and immediately licensed him in canon or civil law, or in both, to teach that field of knowledge by the authority of the pope and in the name of the Holy Trinity. He was then invested with the insignia of his office, the presenting doctor giving him a book and the master's blessing, which was essential to the act. The candidate then seated himself on the magisterial chair, the *cathedra*, and a biretta was placed upon his head and a golden ring upon his finger. The ring seems to have signified either his equality with the knights or his espousal to science. Finally, the presenting doctor gave him "the paternal benediction and the kiss of peace in the name of the Father and of the Son and of the Holy Ghost, Amen."

After these ceremonies were over, if the student were not

[6] Cf. Document 6, Appendix.

too poor, there was a procession through the city, a "triumph" of the new doctor, whose cavalcade was preceded at Bologna by three university pipers and four trumpeters.

In earlier times the gifts to professors and university officials had been robes; later on, these were commuted into money payments, and frequently the exact amount was stipulated in the statutes. Besides the archdeacon and the doctors, there were many minor officials to be remembered, and the whole proceeding was a costly one to the average student. In addition to fees, there were customary presents of a cap, gloves, and a box of candy to each of the doctors and to the archdeacon, while the prior of the college got a ring. At Pisa, the box of candy was specified as a one-pound box! At Bologna each year one poor student was given his doctorate free.

After all these expenses were met, there came the banquet for friends and new colleagues. Some of the wealthier students even went so far as to stage a tournament. At Bologna, however, these were forbidden by statute, and the student had to swear that he would not have such entertainment. The expenses of these amusements were formidable, and the Council of Vienna in 1311 legislated to limit the expenses to "3000 *solidi tournois*." At the Spanish universities these ceremonies of inception were carried on with like solemnity and expense, and sometimes the new doctor provided a bull fight for the amusement of his colleagues and the university!

A DOCTOR OF DIVINITY

The various steps leading to the doctorate in theology were similar to those of the other faculties except that the course

144

for the doctor of theology was much longer. In the Paris decree of 1215, the minimum age of the doctor was given as thirty-five years, and this rule seems to have been kept. St. Thomas Aquinas was under the age of thirty-five when he came up for his doctorate, and a special exception had to be made in his case. In the regulations of the "reform" of 1366, the theology course lasted about sixteen years, and in the statutes of Cardinal d' Estouteville, almost a hundred years later (1452), the course was lessened only by one year. At Oxford, for example, the student spent four years in theological study before he "opposed" in the disputations and six years before he "responded," and this if he were a master in arts already. If he were not a master of arts, it was six years before opponency and eight years before he could respond. The students for opposing and responding at Oxford were taken from those who had not yet lectured and were not yet bachelors. At Paris some have distinguished three separate steps in the bachelor's degree itself; the *biblicus ordinarius*, or the *cursor*, who after some six years of study could present himself before four doctors for an examination, and if successful could enter upon his baccalaureate by giving a course of lectures on some book of the Bible; next the *sententiarius*, who after nine years of study could begin some lectures on Lombard's book of the *Sentences;* the *formati*, or formed bachelors, who had completed their work on the *Sentences* but had to continue to take part in the disputations and scholastic exercises and to deliver a certain number of university sermons.

The distinctions made between the bachelors in theology at the different stages in their academic progress are not always easy to discern in the various universities, but in general the type of preparation was much the same. The antecedent conditions were a certain number of years of theological study centering upon the Bible and the book of the *Sentences* (the manual of theology), the teaching by lecture method of a certain number of the books of the Bible and parts of the *Sentences*, the delivery of some university sermons, and the oppositions and responsions before the bachelors and masters and under various masters. When all these had been accomplished and the applicant had reached the required age of thirty-five years, then there lay between him and his goal of a medieval doctorate in theology three last requirements: the deposition of the master, the license from the chancellor, and the inception itself.

At Paris, for example, there was another examination before the deposition of the master. From the statutes for the theological faculty at Bologna (and these mirror the customs of Paris) we know that the candidate's examination consisted in the statement and defense of two theses assigned him by the dean three days before the examination. Then, at the assembly of the dean and masters, the candidate defended the theses and responded to the arguments brought forward by the various members of the board. When this had been finished, there came the deposition or testimony of the masters as to the morals and the learning of the candidate. Both Gregory IX in the decree of April 13, 1231, and Alexander IV in that of 1255 refer to this practice. According to these decrees all the masters of theology at Paris had to bear witness to the knowledge and good life of the proposed candidate. At Oxford it was decreed that if there was only one regent master in theology, the deposition had also to be made by the non-regent masters. Besides this, the candidate had to be presented to the chancellor by a regent master, who must give special testimony in his behalf. If the deposition was in favor of the man, then the license, or the permission to lecture as a regent master and to exercise all the rights of such a master, would be given. At Oxford the statutes required eighteen masters to "depose" for a candidate for the M.A.; of these at least nine, besides the master who presented him, had to swear that they knew from personal knowledge that the man was qualified, and five had to affirm that they believed him qualified.

After a favorable deposition, the chancellor would grant the licentiate in the following words:

For the honor of Our Lord Jesus Christ, the Blessed Virgin and all the saints, and for the advancement of Holy Church and the *Studium*, I, by my authority and that of the whole university, grant to you the permission of incepting in such and such a faculty, of lecturing (*legendi*) and of disputing and of doing all those things which pertain to the status of a master in the same faculty, when you shall have fulfilled those things which pertain to that solemnity. In the name of the Father and of the Son and of the Holy Spirit, Amen.

"Those things" which had to be fulfilled referred to the last ceremonies of the graduation cycle; namely, the actual inception. We have a considerable amount of data on the way the inception for a theological candidate was handled at Bologna in the fourteenth century, for the statutes are dated 1364. Furthermore, these were modeled closely on Paris and help us to understand the common practices in the various *studia*. There were two separate sections to the theological inception, paralleling that of the arts and other graduations, and both

147

were composed of disputations and lectures. First, there were the disputations known as the "vespers," held on the afternoon of a class day (*dies legibilis*), at which time all other lectures and disputations were suspended so that all masters and students could attend. The candidate chose four questions; two were disputed at vespers and two at the second part of the ceremonies, which at Paris was called the "*aula*" because it took place in the bishop's hall (*aula*). The master who presented the new doctor presided at vespers. In the first disputation the respondent was a bachelor, and the difficulties were proposed by the presiding master first, and then by some of the bachelors. The respondent gave an answer only to the arguments proposed by the master. This was all there was to the first disputation; the candidate himself has not yet entered the lists.

At the second disputation of the vespers, the licentiate, or new doctor, was himself the respondent. The exercise began by arguments pro and con given by a senior master; then the licentiate took over and developed and proved his theses. The master who had given the pro-and-con arguments in the introduction now brought out the heavy artillery with five arguments proving that the defendant's position was erroneous. The licentiate replied only to the first two, and the master "subsumed" on the first two and was again answered by the defendant; and again there was a subsumption—that is, an argument which flows logically from one of the premises of the argument as first advanced and requires further distinction and clarification. Then another master gave four more arguments, and the defendant replied to the first argument. Next the presiding master interrupted proceedings to give a speech in praise of the Holy Scriptures, as well as to recommend the candidate and to announce the day of the *aula* and also the lecture, giving the location of the schoolroom and the particular book on which the new doctor would lecture and thus begin his career.

The second part of these ceremonies, the *aula*, was held in the morning at about nine o'clock, and on this day no other scholastic exercise was permitted. At the ceremonies the new doctor was seated between the chancellor, on his right with the senior masters, and the master who had presided at the vespers, on his left with the junior masters. The master who presided at the *aula* now placed a biretta on the head of the new doctor, who then made a short speech in honor of the Holy Scriptures, and as the first act of his new office directed the disputation which followed. The respondent was a bachelor, who proposed three or four conclusions regarding the third question which the doctor had selected. The new master made four opposing arguments, and the respondent answered the first two and was again answered in this same argument by the new master; they bandied conclusions three times on the first argument and twice on the second. Then the presiding master became the opponent and advanced three objections, with two sub-arguments for the first and one for the second. Finally, the last or fourth question was raised and discussed, and in this exchange only the doctors or masters took part. The senior master proposed the question with arguments both for and against it, and the youngest master answered and determined the question. The oldest master then argued against this determination and was argued with in turn by a younger master. Then another of the senior masters proposed the same

149

question with a different set of proofs and was answered by another junior master with a different set of counter-arguments, and the same tournament of wits proceeded as before.

In conclusion, the new master determined the third question which had been discussed by summing up the various arguments and giving the solution which seemed to him the more reasonable.

This whole cycle of ceremonies was concluded at the first lecture of the new master, which was named the "resumption." At this lecture the new doctor of divinity finished his speech in praise of Holy Scripture which he had left uncompleted in his *aula* and dealt with the second question of the vespers in which he was the respondent. Lastly he returned again to the third question of the four which he had originally chosen to discuss, and with a new respondent proposed and determined it. In this fashion he began his ordinary career as a regent master.

From this survey of the student's progress to the doctorate, it will have been noted that the functions of student and teacher were not separated in the medieval university. Indeed, the newly made doctor or master had already some years of teaching experience which enabled him to appreciate the ability to transfer that learning which he was busily acquiring.

Now that he had become a master or doctor, he had also new duties to perform, should he continue to "profess" the learning he had acquired. His first duty was to lecture and teach (*legere*) in the schools, his second to conduct and share in the various types of disputations (*disputare*). If he were a doctor of divinity, he had the added duty of preaching the university type of sermon, a specialized form of medieval preaching.

The Master as Lecturer

Mention has already been made of the class hours, the schoolrooms, and the type of lecture as well as its length. The lectures were delivered in Latin, and this custom was rigorously kept. In the late fifteenth century, at Paris, the "chirurgeons," or surgeons, were admitted to university medical lectures along with the medical students, but with reservations which irked them. They rebelled against their restricted position, and the medical faculty replied by opening its lectures to the inferior class of "barber-surgeons." To this the surgeons replied by pointing out that the barber-surgeons understood no Latin, and the university statutes forbade the use of any other language. Moreover, the doctors were bound by their oath to obey the university statutes. The doctors solved their dilemma by first lecturing in Latin and then repeating the discourse in the vernacular. This broke the resistance of the surgeons, who admitted their inferior position in relation to that of full medical students and were then received back into favor by the faculty.

Before the student obtained his doctorate in any faculty, he had to lecture on certain books of the subject he was studying and to take part in various disputations with both bachelors and masters. Thus it was to his advantage to acquire a certain amount of teaching notes and outlines as he passed through the various stages of his career. In a famous manuscript information about the preparation and achievement of the theological

151

doctorate, there are examples of the kinds of collections and extracts that a doctoral candidate would make.[7] The theological student would wish to acquire as complete a set of commentaries on the Scriptures and the *Sentences* as he could, plus a whole arsenal of arguments and counter-arguments on which he could draw for his classes and disputations. He would gather a large number of definitions of terms, some of them based on rather fantastic etymology; for instance, the definition of *"sententia"* as *quasi sensum tenentia*! Likewise the future professor would gather a large number of brief questions with their answers, which were evidently gathered with an eye on the examinations, for many of them seem the kind of brief questions which the lecturer would put in class with a single argument pro and con.

This type of note-taking shows us the general methods and objectives of medieval teaching and scholarship. Doctors were striving to teach, and students to obtain, a logical grasp, clear and sharp, of the various questions and problems which came up for discussion. For this purpose they developed their many definitions, divisions, and distinctions. The whole type of Aristotelian commentary perfected in the second half of the thirteenth century, especially in the commentaries of St. Thomas Aquinas, with the tremendous apparatus of analysis and division, distinctions, and subdivisions and further analyses, represents the full development of this technique. As today's college student's notes usually mirror the modern emphasis on factual information, sometimes to the exclusion of much rea-

[7] *Ms. Assisi* 158 which forms the basis for the excellent work of A. G. Little and F. Pelster, S.J., *Oxford Theology and Theologians* (Oxford, 1934).

soning on such information, so these extracts of medieval students give us the picture of their ideal of college training—a sharp, logical knowledge of various problems, but at times lacking in the factual information necessary to orientate its definitions and divisions.

When Odofredus, a famous professor of law at Bologna, announced his course for the next year to the students, he gave us a good picture of the technique in general use:

If you please, I will begin the *Old Digest* (Books 1–28 and first two titles of book 29) on the eighth day or thereabouts after the feast of St. Michael (Sept. 29) and I will finish it entire with all ordinary and extraordinary, by God's help, in the middle of August or thereabouts. The *Code* I will always begin within about a fortnight of the feast of St. Michael and I will finish it with all ordinary and extraordinary, God willing, on the first of August or thereabouts. The extraordinary lectures used not to be given by the doctors. And so all scholars including the unskilled and novices will be able to make good progress with me, for they will hear their text as a whole, nor will anything be left out, as was once done in this region, indeed was the usual practice. For I shall teach the unskilled and novices but also the advanced students. For the unskilled will be able to make satisfactory progress in the position of the case and exposition of the letter; the advanced students can become more learned in the subtleties of questions and opposing opinions. I shall also read all the glosses, which was not done before my time. . . . For it is my purpose to teach you faithfully and in a kindly manner, in which instruction the following order has customarily been observed by my master, which method I shall retain. First, I shall give you the summaries of each title before I come to the text. Second, I shall put forth well and distinctly and in the best terms I can, the purport of each law. Third, I shall read the text in order to correct it. Fourth, I shall briefly restate the meaning. Fifth, I shall solve conflicts, adding general matters (which are commonly called *brocardica*) and subtle and useful distinctions and questions with the solutions, so far as divine Providence shall assist me. And if any law is deserving of a review by reason of its fame or difficulty, I shall reserve it for an afternoon review.[8]

There was an interesting piece of legislation prescribed at Paris on December 10, 1355. The document begins by noting that "there are two methods of lecturing on books in the liberal arts which have been tried; the former masters of philosophy spoke so rapidly that the mind of the auditor could understand but could not keep up with them in writing; the later masters spoke so slowly that the auditors could keep up with them in note-taking; after diligent comparison, the first method is found to be the better"![9] The decree bound all members of the faculty of arts whether masters or scholars, where and whenever lecturing, disputing, or explaining, to follow the first method. They had to swear to do so, and the penalty for non-observance was deprivation for a year "from lecturing and from honors, offices and other advantages of our faculty." Furthermore, if one offended a second time, the penalty was doubled. The document described the "better" method as "so speaking as if no one was taking notes in front of them, in the way that sermons and recommendations are made in the university and which the *lecturers in the other faculties follow.*"

Evidently the faculty of arts at Paris foresaw some violent

[8] Reprinted with permission from Lynn Thorndike, *University Records and Life in the Middle Ages* (New York: Columbia University Press, 1944), pp. 66–67.

[9] Cf. document in Thorndike, *Univ. Records*, pp. 237–238.

objections on the part of the students, for they further stipulated: "Moreover, listeners who oppose the execution of this
our statute by shouting, hissing, noise-making, or throwing
stones by themselves or by their servants and accomplices or
in any other way, we deprive of and cut off from our com-
pany for a year and for each relapse we increase the penalty
double and quadruple. . . ." In 1386 there was a case brought up
at Paris by Aime Dubrueil, a doctor of the *Decretals* (canon
law), who demanded to be allowed to lecture at "matins," or
before dawn, by candle-light and to lecture again at prime,
which was the usual time for the doctors to lecture on the
Decretum. Aime was doing double duty and had therefore a
large number of pupils from which to draw his income. But his
procedure was contrary to the custom by which the bachelors
lectured at the early hour without a candle, and he lost his case.
To make sure that the lectures of the bachelors were both
rapid and *extempore* they used the simple expedient of *making
them lecture in the dark!*

When the doctor had finished his prescribed matter he probably concluded as did Odofredus:

Now, gentlemen, we have begun and finished and gone through
this book as you know who have been in the class, for which we
thank God and His Virgin Mother and all His saints. It is an ancient
custom in this city that when a book is finished Mass should be
sung to the Holy Ghost and it is a good custom and hence should
be observed. But since it is the practice that doctors on finishing
a book should say something of their plans, I will tell you something but not much. Next year I expect to give ordinary lectures
well and lawfully as I always have but no extraordinary lectures,
for students are not good payers, wishing to learn but not to pay,

155

as the saying is: "All desire to know but none to pay the price."
I have nothing more to say to you beyond dismissing you with
God's blessing and begging you to attend the Mass.[10]

THE MASTER AND HIS
INTELLECTUAL TOURNAMENTS

The second duty of the medieval professor was that of "disputing." The disputation in the thirteenth and fourteenth centuries was a most important part of the educational system.
The technique of disputation was zealously developed and perfected not only in the theological faculty but in arts, law, and
medicine. By the thirteenth century the disputation had developed into the formal discussion of a problem between two
or more scholars of whom one was the defender of an opinion
and the other, or others, brought objections and difficulties
against it. Recent research traces the origins of the formal disputation at least as far back as the end of the twelfth century.
During the thirteenth century it reached its perfection and
became general university practice.

Besides the types of disputation connected with the "graduation" ceremonies of both bachelor and master, there was the
frequent disputation conducted by the master in his own
classes. In its simplest form this was the "question in the
schools," when the master would put a question to a student,
who would try to answer it—or the student might be the
questioner. Then, later, a respondent was appointed who had
to give answers or preliminary solutions to the question and

[10] Quoted with permission from C. H. Haskins, *The Rise of the
Universities* (Providence: Brown University, 1923), p. 60.

156

answer the objections brought forth, but he was not the teacher or master.

In the public and "ordinary" disputations, the respondent and opponent were students or bachelors, while the one who summed up and gave the final solutions was the master, who thus "determined" the question. More than one problem might be raised in an "ordinary" disputation, provided that it was connected with the matter. Usually the determination by the master followed immediately, on the same day and in the same general session. The university beadles went around to the classes to invite students to these ordinary disputations, to which, it seems, the regent masters did not come but only their students and bachelors. In Paris, for example, attendance at them in the faculty of theology was compulsory for the "formed bachelors"—that is, those who had finished their lecture work on the *Sentences*. Ordinary disputations seem to have been held frequently; at Oxford in the medical faculty, the rules call for weekly disputations, and in the faculty of arts the new master was to dispute on every "disputable day" for forty continuous days. At Oxford, however, not every ordinary disputation was followed by a full determination.

A second type of disputation, which was more of a rarity, was the disputation *de quolibet*, the "disputation-about-any-thing-you-please." The origins of this form of disputation are still obscure, but by the time of St. Thomas this disputation *de quolibet* was held annually at Paris in the second week of Advent and from the fourth week of Lent to Palm Sunday. The disputation *de quolibet* differed from the ordinary disputation in that the subjects chosen had a greater range and variety, frequently being topics warmly debated in the schools

157

at the time; and in that participants included masters, bachelors, and distinguished visitors. Because the presiding master was under fire from the clever arguments of his colleagues, or perhaps from visiting professors, the disputation *de quolibet* required considerable skill and knowledge. The determination of the presiding master was given on another day, thus affording him a chance to sleep on the difficulties and see what distinctions the next morning might bring.

Although the art of disputation, so sedulously cultivated during the days of medieval universities, came in for much criticism from writers during the following centuries, recent research has tended to a more moderate opinion. The ordeal of answering the questions of other professors, equally skilled in the learning of the age and familiar with the problems through long years of study and discussion, was not an easy one. Today it would surely be an advantage in any faculty to have the opportunity to hear masters and graduate students questioning and answering one another about problems in their specialized fields. It would also be good training for graduate students to defend their opinions publicly before colleagues or masters during their course of study. The medieval scholar always believed that "nothing was fully understood unless it was first chewed by the teeth of disputation."

THE THEOLOGICAL MASTER
AS PREACHER

One of the formulas for granting the license in theology runs as follows: (The chancellor) "by the authority of Al-

158

mighty God and the apostles Peter and Paul and the apostolic see, gives to them" (the licentiates) "the permission to dispute and to lecture and to preach. . . ." Thus, the three duties of the *theological* master are summarized. He had to lecture, to dispute, and to preach.

At Paris the custom was to give a more solemn type of sermon in the morning; and in the afternoon or evening of the same day, a shorter version of the same, termed a collation (*collatio*). The collation seems to have been a kind of résumé or a type of practice sermon which bachelors in theology were required to give as an indication of their ability to preach. The number of these university sermons was large, since they were not only given on each Sunday but on many feast days.

In the manuals of instruction for the writers of medieval sermons, the preacher is advised to give useful talks, to instruct and not merely to charm his audience, to keep to his text, and to bolster his arguments with good and reputable authorities. He was also advised to use moderate language, to avoid vulgar jokes, and to steer between a sermon that was too childish and one too abstruse for his audience. These were general norms suitable for any sermon preacher; but when the authors treat of the university sermon, then the detailed regulations approach oratorical bureaucracy. The medieval university sermon was a complex affair, as a brief description of some aspects of it will indicate.

In Robert Baseborn's treatise on preaching, *Forma Praedicandi*,[11] there is a chapter which enumerates twenty-two different parts in the university sermon, the last seven of them be-

11 This treatise is to be found in P. Charland's *Artes Praedicandi* (Ottawa, 1936).

longing more properly to what we would call rhetorical ornaments. A brief description of the first fifteen gives some idea of the technique:

Thematis inventio. This was what a modern preacher would refer to as his text, and its choice and the number of clauses it might contain were regulated. Generally it had to be taken from the books of the Bible; neither the wording nor sense could be changed.

Auditus allectio. This was the prescribed form for citing the text for the benefit of the listeners.

Prothema. This was an introduction to the prayer which was next inserted and invited the hearers to join in saying it. A good example of what is meant by a *prothema* is the introduction to the *Pater Noster* in the Canon of the Mass in the Roman missal. The *prothema* had also, in some way or other, to restate the main text of the sermon, and so has been compared to the minor theme in a symphonic movement.

Oratio. The prayer was said to gain the blessing of God for a good delivery by the speaker and a good reception by the audience. The speaker would include a petition in this formula such as "Peace be to you" (*Pax vobis*), to which the audience would make the proper answer.

Thematis introductio. After the prayer there was another repetition of the text, presented in the same formula as before. The preacher was advised to do this so that those of his listeners who came late would know what he was talking about. He must take care that this paragraph should catch the attention of the audience.

Thematis divisio. The text was next taken part by part, and the speaker formally announced the number of divisions. Two or three main divisions were allowable; four were reckoned to smack of vanity. To substantiate his division, the speaker must line up two or three reputable authorities, and in the statement presenting the division of the divided text, there were rules for consonance, assonance, and rhyme. There was also cadence required in this phase of the sermon.

Partium declaratio and *Partium confirmatio*. In these two sections the divisions of the sermon were more fully explained. The declaration was the proof from reason for the preacher's division, and the confirmation offered scriptural authority for it.

Dilatatio. This was the main part of the sermon, the extended treatment of the subject.

Digressio. This was a side-development from the main theme but connected with it. A digression was not supposed to be longer than the *dilatatio*, but there was apparently no precise specification as to the number of digressions.

Correspondentia. During this part of the sermon the preacher went back to his first division and showed the relationship of the various parts. There was also a *Correspondentiae congruentia*, in which he brought out the interrelations of the various subdivisions of the main divisions.

Circulatio. This was a restatement of the original parts in a different order and explanation.

Convolutio. This was another restatement, this time of the subdivisions, and it involved a comparison with the original divisions in which another, and new, set of relationships was set up.

Unitio. This followed the above step and was a general union of the various parts of the sermon, leading up to the conclusion.

Clausio. This was the conclusion, which must be drawn from the original language of the text.

It will be readily admitted that this type of university sermon is a complicated affair. There is, however, a similarity to the classroom lecture with its divisions and subdivisions or the

161

type of professorial activity which is found in the various disputations of medieval university life. Thus, the thesis with its divisions and subdivisions, its proofs and distinctions, is paralleled in the medieval university sermon. Some have compared the medieval sermon to plain chant, for in both, although the rules are complex and intricate, the result is a work of art. Doubtless, to the medieval university students versed in the art of definition and division, this type of sermon was not only informational and inspirational but artistic and beautiful. Some might say that there was a Gothic type of sermon as well as a Gothic type of architecture. Today most of us would probably prefer the architecture.

ADDITIONAL READINGS

Charland, T. M., *Artes Praedicandi* (Paris and Ottawa, 1936).

Haskins, C. H., "The Medieval Professor," *The Rise of the Universities* (New York, 1923), now in paperback.

Kibre, P., *Nations in the Mediaeval European Universities*, Mediaeval Academy of America, Publication No. 49 (Cambridge, Mass., 1948).

Little, A. G., and Pelster, F., *Oxford Theology and Theologians* (Oxford, 1934).

Post, Gaines, "Masters, Salaries and Student-Fees in Mediaeval Universities," *Speculum*, VII (1932), 181–198.

Rashdall, H., Powicke, F. M., Emden, A. B., *The Universities of Europe in the Middle Ages* (Oxford, 1936), 3 vols.

Thorndike, L., *University Records and Life in the Middle Ages*, University of Columbia, Records of Civilization, XXXVIII (New York, 1944).

V. STUDENTS: THEIR PRIVILEGES
AND PROBLEMS

STUDENT PRIVILEGES

One of the characteristics distinguishing the medieval student was the place he occupied in medieval society. He enjoyed a number of privileges, some of which have been lost to modern students; indeed, some of them might not be considered *privileges* today.

An early and important document granting and confirming privileges to scholars was that of Emperor Frederick I (1152–1190), dated 1158.[1] This charter, which may have been intended for the student class in general and not merely for Bologna students, was confirmed by Pope Alexander III (1159–1181) in the usual fashion in which emperor and pope, or king and pope, co-operated in the promotion of the medieval university. In general, the decree granted to the student the choice, as defendant, of being cited before either his bishop or his own master, and by this it established the privilege for the student of an exemption from local civil courts. Kings and popes took under their protection the students as a special class, and confirmations of this privilege to be tried in what would usually be a more "friendly" court than that of the townsmen were

[1] Cf. Norton, *Readings in the History of Education*, pp. 85 ff. Cf. *supra*, p. 26.

163

frequently renewed. For example, Philip Augustus of France (1180–1223) granted and confirmed to Paris University students privileges of this type in 1200.

Authorities strove to protect students in their travels to and from the universities:

> . . . We in our loving-kindness do grant to all scholars who are traveling for the sake of study and especially to professors of divine and sacred laws, this privilege: Both they and their messengers are to come in security to the places in which the studies are carried on and there they are to abide in security. . . .[2]

In addition to the privilege of being cited before an ecclesiastical court, Innocent IV (1243–1254) exempted the Parisian students from citation to ecclesiastical courts outside of Paris, so that their studies would not be interrupted:

> . . . To the masters and scholars at Paris. So that you can carry on with your studies more freely and be less occupied with other affairs, we grant your request and by the authority of this present letter grant you the privilege of not being summoned by apostolic letters beyond the limits of the city of Paris regarding questions that have arisen within the city limits unless there is express mention of this privilege.[3]

This privilege was a distinct one from the privilege of exemption from secular jurisdiction (*privilegium fori*) and was designated by the Latin tag of *jus non trahi extra*, "the right of not being summoned outside." It became characteristic of all the universities which were influenced by Paris University customs.

[2] Norton, *op. cit.*, p. 82.
[3] *Ibid.*, p. 87.

Another important privilege which the medieval student enjoyed was that of tax exemption. In the beginning it was a personal privilege, but later it was applied to the university corporation as a whole. A charter, granted by Philip VI (1328–1350) of France in 1340–1341, decrees in part:

To the aforesaid Masters and Scholars (of Paris) now in attendance at the university, and to those who are hereafter to come to the same university, or who are actually preparing in sincerity so to come, also while (they are) staying at the university, or returning to their own homes, we grant . . . that no layman, of whatever condition or prominence he may be, whether he be a private person, prefect or bailiff, shall disturb, molest, or presume otherwise in any way whatsoever to seek to extort anything from the aforesaid masters and scholars in person, family or property, under pretext of toll, *tallia* (special type of tax), tax customs, or any such personal taxes, or other personal exaction of any kind, while they are either coming to the university itself, or actually preparing in sincerity to come, or returning to their own homes; and whose status as scholars shall be established by the proper oath.[4]

This exemption from taxation was also extended to those who were working for the university corporation as bailiffs, servitors, and the like. Disputes about this privilege sometimes had to be settled by royal authority, as for example, when Henry VI of England in 1450 ruled on the matter for the University of Caen in Normandy.[5]

Besides privileges granted by king, emperor, or pope, the students sometimes were able to win important privileges from

[4] Norton, *op. cit.*, p. 89.
[5] Cf. document in Norton, *op. cit.*, p. 105.

165

the townsmen. One of the early migrations from the university of Bologna had led the students to form another university at Padua in 1222, but a large group, dissatisfied with the conditions offered them there, drew up a contract with the city fathers of Vercelli. By this contract of 1228, Vercelli townsmen agreed to turn over five hundred of the best houses of the city to the *studium* and to fix a rent ceiling, the actual amount to be determined by a group of representatives from the city and the university-to-be. They also agreed to lend a certain amount of money to the students at a fixed rate of interest and to pay the salaries of one theologian, three doctors of civil law, four canon lawyers, two medical doctors, two dialecticians, and two grammarians. These masters were to be elected by the rectors and to teach free of charge. They also contracted to provide two scribes, or copyists, who would copy books for the students at fixed rates, to grant certain exemptions from local taxation, and to send messengers to other parts of Italy to announce the foundation of the new university.

Besides indicating what terms the students could obtain from townsmen, the contract also gives information on the number of students at the time, for Padua was an offshoot of Bologna.

Another example of a municipal grant is seen in the relations of the students with the citizens during the revival of studies at Padua in 1260–1262. The university at Padua had fallen on hard days during the period 1237–1260 when the city was in the hands of a tyrannical government. In 1260, however, the city regained its freedom, and there was an increase in the university enrollment, due to a group which came from Bologna, where university studies were suffering from the war between

Bologna and Forlì and the interdict on the Bologna schools. The new agreement stated that the salaries of a certain number of professors were to be paid by the city and made the lending of money to students easier.

Graduates of Paris, Bologna, and Oxford were generally recognized to have a degree which entitled them to teach anywhere in the world. This privilege was termed the *jus ubique docendi* ("the right of teaching everywhere") and gradually became one of the usual clauses in the formal document legally constituting a university. Sometimes this privilege was granted long after a university had become a recognized institution of learning. The papal document or bull which was issued at the founding of the University of Toulouse in 1233 contained the formula, and this particular document became a model for later grants of privileges. Not all universities, however, were willing to accept a professor from another university into their faculty just because this clause occurred in his diploma. Certainly both Paris and Oxford were chary of allowing others to enter their professorial ranks without some exhibition of competence. They might demand a disputation before the other faculty members, which was one of the types called the "resumption" (*resumptio*).

A most important university privilege referred to the university as a whole corporation and would be called, in modern terms, "the right of the university to go on strike" (*cessatio*). The *cessatio* was a dangerous weapon, as some towns or cities discovered to their sorrow, when their local university, bag and baggage, departed for greener pastures. Usually, the right of suspending lectures until redress was granted was used against either civil or ecclesiastical authorities with whom the university was at odds. Often the dispute originated in the

167

wranglings of the students with some tavern keeper about the price of wine or beer, or in some small street fight between a foreign student and a townsman. Although of small importance in origin, these petty quarrels developed into important controversies about the relative position of the university in medieval society and sometimes resulted in the bestowal or clarification of important university privileges.

The privilege of *cessatio* was conferred by Pope Gregory IX in his famous document of 1231 regarding the University of Paris. He lists among the reasons why the university may suspend its lectures such things as the following: refusal of the right to fix ceiling-prices for lodgings, an injury or mutilation of a student for which suitable satisfaction had not been given within fifteen days, the unlawful imprisonment of a student. "Unless the injury ceases when you remonstrate, you may, if you judge it wise, suspend your lectures immediately."[6]

The sudden departure of hundreds, or perhaps of thousands, of students from the relatively small medieval cities was a seriout threat to such cities' economic growth and health, and the fact that the medieval university did not have a large group of buildings of its own, but merely rented various halls and lodgings, made this event a distinct possibility. Often enough, other cities would take advantage of such a quarrel to offer the students better terms and tenements. During the great cessation at Paris in 1229, the English king, Henry III, sent the following invitation across the channel:

Greeting to the masters and the whole body of scholars at Paris. Humbly sympathizing with the exceeding tribulations and dis-

---

[6] Cf. document in Thorndike, *Univ. Records*, pp. 35–39.

tresses which you have suffered at Paris under an unjust law, we wish by our pious aid, with reverence to God and His holy Church, to restore your status to its proper condition of liberty. Wherefore we have concluded to make known to your entire body that if it shall be your pleasure to transfer yourselves to our kingdom of England and to remain there to study we will for this purpose assign to you cities, boroughs, towns, whatsoever you may wish to select, and in every fitting way cause you to rejoice in a state of liberty and tranquility which should please God and fully meet your needs.[7]

Had the Parisian dons decided to emigrate and had they selected London for their habitation, the might-have-beens in English history become most interesting.

This right of *cessatio* was *the* great weapon of the medieval universities, but owing to the growth of endowed colleges in the fifteenth and sixteenth centuries and to the rise of the strong national monarchies, the university lost the power to use it. With the loss of this power, the gradual subordination of the university to either local or national pressures became more evident as the medieval period closed and the modern era began.

THE NEW STUDENT ARRIVES AT
HIS UNIVERSITY

Before the college system became a common part of the universities, the new student would have to seek out living-quarters for himself. The university would have certain suggestions to make; there would probably be one or two board-

[7] Quoted from Norton, *op. cit.*, p. 95.

inghouses whose proprietors had refused to keep to the rents fixed by the university, and these houses would be forbidden. Quite possibly, the new student would have some friend or acquaintance at the university on whose experience and knowledge as an "old boy" he could rely. If he were a poor student, his room and furnishings would be meager indeed; if he were of the nobility, he would have better lodgings, and perhaps a special servant.

If the new student had enrolled in a university like Bologna where the student universities controlled so much of campus life, he would have placed his name on the roll of the ultramontane university and English nation, supposing an English student, and have made the various promises demanded of new members. With these accomplished, he would be under the protecting arm of the student university; and although he could not partake of Bolognese citizenship, the power of the student university would make up for this deficiency. If he were in Paris or one of the universities following the Parisian model, he would find that the nations were organizations of masters and not students, at least as far as the arts college went, and his first need then would be to find himself a master under whom to pursue his studies.

The finding of a master would not be difficult, as masters were much interested in being found. Very likely, the new student would not have been around long before he was approached by some friend of a master who would endeavor to sign him up for that teacher. One of the thirteenth-century manuals of advice to students stresses the importance of a little experimentation before selection, and the student is advised to go to the professor's classes *for three days before making up his mind*. At Bologna, according to the statutes of the arts faculty, any student could attend any class for the space of fifteen days before he could be charged for attendance. Odofredus, some of whose remarks have already been quoted, emphasized the importance for the new student of a careful selection of the master under whom he wished to begin his career.

Soon after arrival, the freshman often experienced some "hazing." In the *Manuale Scholarium*[8] (probably written about 1480, but certainly giving us information about customs of long standing), we find a picture of university life at Heidelberg. The little work has some eighteen chapters and "conducts the student from his matriculation to his degree, and informs him by the way on many subjects quite unnecessary for either." The young man pictured in this "manual of scholars who propose to attend universities and profit therein" is apparently from a moderately well-to-do family and has serious intentions of studying. His hazing as a freshman is lengthily described. The "frosh," or *beanus*, is treated as if he were a stinking beast with horns and tusks; there is a great ceremonial at which these are removed, and he is subjected to some rather violent horseplay.

In the other chapters of the manual we get some glimpses of ordinary student life; the quarrels with room-mates, conversations in Latin, letters from home (but without the hoped-for money enclosure), the student who is reported for breaking

[8] There is a conversational English translation by R. F. Seybolt, *The Manuale Scholarium* (Cambridge, Mass., 1921).

171

the university statutes, who falls in love and out again, who borrows money from his room-mate, and so on. Finally the student is described as receiving a letter from his parents telling him it is high time he took his degree and came home. This news comes as a sad surprise and disturbs him mightily, for he has attended few lectures and has made several enemies among the professors. What shall he do? His own master discourages him from attempting the final examinations, but the other speaker in this dialogue encourages him to write home for more money, give a great feast for the professors, distribute his money and gifts judiciously and rest confident that all will go well. Apparently, at least in the book, all did go well, for the manual concludes with the forms of invitation to the inception banquet.

Another medieval manual, entitled *De Disciplina Scholarium*, claims to be a portrayal of Athenian university customs in the fifth century! It seems to mirror much better the medieval customs. It was a popular book from the thirteenth century to the seventeenth, as is proved by the more than thirty printed editions of it, from 1482 to 1633. In advising the more advanced students, the writer points out the various hindrances to study, among them such things as unrestrained indulgence in sensual pleasures, the danger of too much wine, the great obstacle of fickleness of mind.

An example of this latter type of student is given: the collegian who was never constant, but like a bird flitted from one thing to another, spending now a month on the satirists, now a day with the historians. Then he turns to rhetoric, and next studies for a month the philosophical works. At last he gives up the matter of studies to become a merchant, but the bilge water sickens, and the seas terrify, him, and he next decides to take up gardening. Failing that, he goes into the army, but on the first enemy attack he flees from the business of war. The idle student is also described at length as a frequenter of taverns and worse, wasting his money and time in wandering about the city, but never consorting with his books. He is characterized by a roving eye, an unrestrained tongue, a disordered visage, and a freakish mind.

The author of the *Disciplina* also tells us of the serious scholars, of whom he has seen many at "Athens." He quotes approvingly the rules for study of Robert de Sorbon (1201–1274). First, the student is advised to dedicate a certain hour to a specified piece of reading and to fix his attention on what he is going to read and not pass on to something else lightly, "for there is the same difference between mere reading and studying as there is between a host and a friend, between a salute exchanged in the street and an unalterable affection." The student should also extract each day, one thought, one truth, and engrave it in his memory with special care. He should be sure to write down summaries, "for unwritten words are blown away as dust before the wind." He should join with his companions in disputations or talk over the class matters with them in familiar conversation, for this helps to clear up the various doubts that have been left in the mind after reading. Lastly, the medieval student is exhorted to prayer, which "avails much for learning." The good student should imitate Christ among the doctors of the Law, by hearing many masters, always seeking out the best students, and not paying regard merely to fame or place of birth. Furthermore, he should

173

listen as well as ask questions, and not be like those students who cry out before the end of the sentence, "I know what you mean."

THE STUDENT AS PORTRAYED IN
LETTERS AND SERMONS

Because letter-writing was not within the scope of everyone's ability, there were in the Middle Ages "professors of correspondence," who practiced and taught the art of official letter-writing and even private correspondence. These *dictatores*, as they were called, taught in the schools or chanceries or took to the road with their knowledge of letter-writing, an art "often and exceeding necessary for the clergy, for monks suitable, and for laymen honorable." They advocated a very formalized type of letter, generally in five parts: the salutation (each medieval class had its own special greeting); the *exordium*, which was to render the reader benevolent; the statement, or narration, of the letter; the petition, which generally took the form of a conclusion from the *exordium* as a major, and narration as a minor, premise in the epistolary syllogism; and finally, the proper phrases of the conclusion.[9]

The complicated construction of the medieval letter demanded more than ordinary skill, and the result was the wholesale copying of letters, as well as the editing of hundreds of "model" letters of various types, put out in correspondence

[9] Cf. C. H. Haskins, *Studies in Medieval Culture* (Oxford, 1929), pp. 1–36, on which the following pages largely depend. These and subsequent quotations are made with permission of Oxford University Press.

copybooks. Real or fictitious letters might thus be drawn upon. For the historian of diplomatics, such models, since they are offered as examples, are open to serious question. But for the historian of customs and medieval society, they can be a true source of information, particularly if the conditions they describe are found so generalized that it is evident that they were commonplaces. Such is the case in the various collections of letters from students to their parents. These mention the various universities of Bologna, Naples, Vienna, Prague, Oxford, Orleans, and Paris. Some are written in a popular Latin, others are quite stiff and formalized; but all of them picture to us the student problems of the Middle Ages. Often, were the letter in English, or some other modern language, and the date-line contemporary, it might be mistaken for that of a present-day student.

The preponderant item in the letters from students to their parents or relatives is not news but *cash*. One father says in a model letter that the student's first song is a demand for money.[10] How to sugar-coat this ever-present pill was the most difficult task facing the letter-writer. Generally the student describes his situation at some center of learning, himself as well and happy, but in great need of money for books and other necessary expenses, as in this example supposedly written from Oxford:

B. to his venerable master A., greeting. This is to inform you that I am studying at Oxford with the greatest diligence, but the matter of money stands greatly in the way of my promotion, as it is now two months since I spent the last of what you sent me. The city is expensive and makes many demands; I have to rent lodg-

[10] Haskins, *op. cit.*, p. 7.

ings, buy necessaries, and provide for many other things which I cannot now specify. Wherefore I respectfully beg your paternity by the promptings of divine pity you may assist me, so that I may be able to complete what I have well begun. For you must know that without Ceres and Bacchus, Apollo grows cold. . . .[11]

Sometimes the student asked for the things he needed directly from home rather than for money to purchase them, as in a twelfth-century letter from Chartres in which two brothers ask their mother for "some thick lambskin for winter clothes, parchment for a psalter, some good chalk, and finally, for Papa's great boots." At times the students attributed their plight to the higher cost of living due to a bad winter, a threatened siege, or a crop failure; or sometimes they laid the blame on a previous messenger who had run away with the money. One letter purports to come from some scholars writing from the dungeon of a prison where they were living on hard and mouldy bread, drinking water bitter with their own tears, and surrounded with a darkness so dense they could feel it. In another, a lad writes to his sister (because he is afraid to write home to his parents) that he is without a blanket to cover him, without shoes or shirt—will she send him clothes and money? The good sister, horrified at his plight, sends him money and some cloth, but cautions him not to tell her husband, because if he hears of it she's "as good as dead."

Not all the answering letters contained only money; many inclosed advice on how *not* to spend it; the student is advised to recall how his Uncle John got along well enough on much less *per diem;* he must remember the needs of the others in the family; or he is told that he should be at home helping his

11 Haskins, *op. cit.,* p. 10.

parents make money, and not extorting it from them by letter. Sometimes the father or guardian had apparently received a quite different report about the student from that contained in the student's own letter, and the response would be somewhat like the following:

To his son G. residing at Orleans, P. of Besançon sends greeting with paternal zeal. It is written, "he also that is slothful in his work is brother to him that is a great waster." I have recently discovered that you live dissolutely and slothfully, preferring license to restraint and play to work and strumming a guitar while the others are at their studies, whence it happens that you have read but one volume of law while your more industrious companions have read several. Wherefore I have decided to exhort you herewith to repent utterly of your dissolute and careless ways, that you may no longer be called a waster and that your shame may be turned to good repute.[12]

Sometimes the student did include some bits of news, or at least some description of his student life, as the following letter shows:

To their very dear and respected parents M. Martre, knight and his wife, M. and S. their sons send greetings and filial obedience. This is to inform you that, by divine mercy, we are living in good health in the city of Orleans and are devoting ourselves wholly to study, mindful of the words of Cato, "to know anything is praiseworthy, etc." We occupy a good and comely dwelling, next door but one to the schools and marketplace, so that we can go to school every day without wetting our feet. We have also good companions in the house with us, well advanced in their studies and of excellent habits—an advantage which we well appreciate, for as the Psalmist

[12] Haskins, *op. cit.*, p. 15.

says, "With an upright man thou wilt show thyself upright." Wherefore lest production cease from lack of material, we beg your paternity to send us by the bearer B., money for buying parchment, ink, a desk, and the other things which we need, in sufficient amount that we may suffer no want on your account (God forbid!) but finish our studies and return home with honor. The bearer will also take charge of the shoes and stockings which you have to send us, and any news at all.[13]

From the various letters it would seem that the journey to the university was not always a happy one, despite the privileges accorded to the traveling student by emperor, king, or pope. Evidently the medieval highwaymen did not respect the student's love of knowledge any more than they did the merchant's love of gain. One letter tells of a student who in crossing the Alps on his way to Bologna was robbed of his clothes, horses, books, and money, and forced to take refuge in a nearby monastery to await further subsidization. Another on his way to Paris joined a group of four fellow travelers only to find that they were robbers who had disguised themselves as clerics.

Once the student arrived at his chosen place of study, according to these letters, he was loath to quit the student life. There are letters of petition for an extension of time for study, no matter what the reason for return home might be; despite the death of loved ones, the difficulties of dividing the inheritance, the danger of war, the student always pleads for permission to remain a little longer at his books. One student of Siena received word that he should return home to marry and that the selected spouse was a good match; he replied that one can always get a wife, but that science once forsaken can-

13 Haskins, *op. cit.*, p. 17.

not be regained. There was the ever-present problem of securing books, which cost so much more than modern ones. There was not only the question of the text itself, but the glosses which had to be copied in a large and readable hand. A student of Orleans wrote home that he had become a famous dialectician, and that he would like to study theology. His father, however, wrote back that, although he praised his ambition, he could not afford the cost of a Bible, and his son should turn his thoughts to a more lucrative profession.

Many of the letters describe the expense of taking a degree, with special emphasis on the inception banquet. A student of Paris wrote to a friend asking him to explain to his father how it was that after he had studied so much, now nothing was lacking but the money for the graduation ceremonies, "for the simple lay mind does not grasp such things"! There were also the letters written home to describe the successful graduation ceremonies, as this model letter of Buoncompagno, a professor of Bologna and author of several rhetorical works, testifies:

Sing unto the Lord a new song, praise him with stringed instruments and organs, rejoice upon the high-sounding cymbals, for your son has held a glorious disputation, which was attended by a great number of teachers and scholars. He answered all questions without a mistake. Moreover, he celebrated a famous banquet, at which both rich and poor were honored as never before, and he has duly begun to give lectures which are already so popular that others' classrooms are deserted and his own are filled.[14]

According to the picture painted in the average letter, the student of the medieval university was diligent and studious,

[14] Haskins, *op. cit.*, p. 28.

went usually to three lectures a day and strove to excel even the professors in his grasp of knowledge. Buoncompagno has a letter for the student who studies too much—who rises in the morning before the bell, comes to school before his fellow students and leaves after all others have departed; at other times stays in his room to study; meditates his lectures at meal time, and even argues in his sleep. But the author also adds that the same form letter could be sent as irony to one who does not take his university work very seriously!

Another source of information on the daily life of the medieval student is the medieval sermon. This type of information, however, must be used with great caution, for the purpose of the preacher was not to write history but to convert a soul. The various sermons of preachers in or near universities with the examples which they use to illustrate their doctrine and keep their hearers awake frequently give us a glimpse into the evil side of student activities. There is the instance of the conceited and proud master whose vain boasts about his prowess in explication of difficult texts caused him to be struck dumb on the very morning of his lecture, and it was with the greatest difficulty that he relearned the seven penitential psalms. The gambling students who do not hesitate to gamble even in church, the wine-bibbers and drunkards, the frequenters of taverns and houses of ill-fame, the violent students ever ready for a street fight and armed only with a knife and without helmet, rushing into a fray that even an armed knight would have sense enough to avoid—these are all described.

Various student attitudes are portrayed for us in these sermons. In one example three Flemish students discuss their future; one plans to become a Cistercian monk, another desires a master's chair at Paris, the third decides for the career of a jongleur. There is the poor student whose only friend is St. Nicholas, and who copies for himself or for others those glosses and texts so necessary for study; but, though he copies correctly, others copy more rapidly and in a better hand. Then there are the rich students who have beautiful books which they never even open.

The masters also come in for their share of castigation. Some teach before they know enough. Copying their lectures from books of others and not drawing on personal knowledge, *they* have to pay the students to come to their classes. Others there are whose sole desire is a crowded classroom, and to obtain it they do not scruple to teach unusual and strange doctrines, and on Sunday or holy days. There are the indulgent masters who allow their students to sleep late and amuse themselves in going about the city, and sometimes they connive at their charges' worst vices. There is also mention of the master who desires not to instruct others but to be thought learned, and who speaks in an obscure manner in order to be thought profound!

The Early Colleges

It would be both pleasant and profitable if in scholastic fashion one could begin the description of the rise and progress of the college system with a clear, concise definition of a college. But this is not easily done, for like many other words in our educational vocabulary the term "college" was used of an earlier and different educational organization. In its educa-

181

tional sense the word "college" could be defined as a "society formed for the purpose of study or instruction." Even with this vague and general definition there is difficulty, because very early colleges were not intended to furnish instruction but were rather places to live—to eat and sleep in, thus giving students more leisure for study and intellectual progress.

Colleges were not peculiar to English university life, for there were many colleges at Paris and at the Italian universities as well. In fact, the earliest colleges were those of Paris, and it would seem that it was from Paris that the other European universities caught the idea. But the development of colleges in England was more pronounced, and later they became more independent than, and somewhat different from, those on the Continent.

Student conditions at the universities help to explain college origins. The average age of the arts freshmen in the medieval university was, as we have said, probably about fifteen or sixteen. Many came from afar and had to live for several years away from home and from the domestic environment which they had known up to that time. Naturally parents would be anxious to insure some kind of good hostel for their sons during these years. There were many dangers in a great medieval city like Paris for the simple youth coming up from the country district, dangers not only of wasted study time, of discouragement and disgust at the program which had appeared at first so interesting, but dangers to moral character —never lacking in any age. As a result, even before the foundation of the college system, there was the natural development of a student-house or hospice (*hospicium*) under the eye of the university officials and inhabited by students very often from the same part of Europe, speaking the same language and having some bond of common understanding. The nation system at Paris would seem at first sight to offer a solution to the housing problem by the very fact that it grouped its various students according to nationality or place of origin; but since at Paris the nation system was reserved for the masters, these nations would not be so helpful as those at the University of Bologna. In general it can be said that, in origins at least, the college was an endowed residence hall, or if not a separate building it was at least a certain number of beds to be provided for a certain number of students in an already existing hospital or hostel. Perhaps the best way to gain some notion of these early colleges is to note the circumstances under which some of the outstanding and oldest ones were founded.

The earliest college-foundation at Paris was a very simple one. Near the cathedral of Notre Dame there was a building known as "The Hospital of Blessed Mary of Paris" or more commonly called the Hôtel-Dieu. It had been the custom in this hospital to set aside a single room for some poor cleric or student, and in the year 1180 a gentleman by the name of Jocius de Londoniis, who had just returned from a pilgrimage to Jerusalem, paid a visit to the hospital and determined to secure a room which would be large enough to support eighteen clerical students. The administrators of the hospital agreed with the benefactor to supply the eighteen students with sufficient beds. It is not clear that everybody got his own bed; there were to be "sufficient" beds. Thus this first college was a very simple affair; its scholars were under no special type of regulation or discipline beyond that enforced upon the ordinary members and inmates of the hospital. Their only duty was

183

to take turns in carrying the cross and holy water at the funerals of those who died in the house, and at night they were bound to say the customary prayers as well as the seven penitential psalms. By the year 1231 this simple college had become an independent community established in a house of its own near the church of St. Christopher, and it was henceforth known as the College of the Eighteen (Collège des Dixhuit).[15] This college lasted from 1180 to 1789, when it was consolidated with other small colleges into what was called the Collège de Louis-le-Grand. The college statutes of 1330 required "a Mass and vigils for Joncio de Londoniis who founded this house."

Another example of an early college is that of the "Good Children of St. Honoré," founded in 1208–1209 by Etienne Belot (or Berot) and his wife. This college was to contain thirteen beds, and again the number of people who could be housed under the vague caption of thirteen beds is not clear. This college was not attached to a religious hospital, but the students were placed under the government of the chapter of the church of St. Honoré. It is not known whether these students were mere grammarians or students in one of the other faculties, nor what type of disciplinary regulations they were to follow. Nor is it evident that in the beginning they were supervised by a master, although they were certainly so supervised in later times.

A different type of college was founded by Robert de Sorbon, canon of Cambrai and afterwards of Paris.[16] His college was for men who were already masters of arts and who

---

[15] Cf. document in Thorndike, *Univ. Records*, pp. 21–22.
[16] Cf. document in Thorndike, *Univ. Records*, pp. 88–98.

wanted to enter upon the long and difficult career which would gain them the coveted doctorate in theology. In the beginning the House of the Sorbonne, as his college was called, was intended for sixteen students of theology, four to be chosen from each of the four nations. Later on, the numbers were increased to thirty-six. Besides these "bursars," who were supported in full at the Sorbonne, there were additional students who were given board and lodging in return for some service performed for the more fully supported bursars. Later on each fellow had a poorer student as his personal attendant who shared his room. Although the bursars had some share in the government of the house, they were far from independent. The archdeacon and chancellor of Paris, doctors of theology and deans of the other two superior faculties, as well as the rectors and proctors of the university all formed the supreme governing body. It would seem, however, that the ordinary administration of the house was left to a provisor, who was not a member of the community but an ecclesiastic who governed it from the outside. The internal officer who presided over the society was elected every year and was entitled prior, or *lator rotuli*, while the financial administration was in the hands of four proctors. The college of the Sorbonne, then, was founded to perpetuate a body of professional theologians at the University of Paris who were not members of the mendicant orders.

As on the Continent, so in England, the problem of housing students at the universities was a thorny one. For the university was in effect an assembly of resident doctors or masters engaged in teaching. For the general way of life of the students, for their lodging and their board, the university assumed little responsibility, though sometimes such problems were forced upon its attention by riots between scholars and townspeople. Although various hostels appeared through the private initiative of masters of arts who hired houses for themselves and students under their direction, there was no set system of such organizations. As the university grew, it became more and more important that some such college system be worked out. Younger students were provided for to some extent in the various hostels, but the older ones who remained to study for the degree of doctor in one of the higher faculties had no special accommodations provided for them. It was precisely this problem which Walter de Merton recognized and attempted to solve when (about 1250) he founded a society of senior students within the university who lived together and who were sufficiently endowed and possessed a type of self-government and a common seal. These scholars, when they had taken their degree, entered into the government of the university. During the decades following Merton's foundation, several other colleges of this type were founded, and soon it became evident that the senior members of the university body had been provided for.

Nothing of a similar type, however, had developed for the younger students—those students in arts who were sometimes only fifteen years old when they came up to the university to begin their studies. It was this problem which William of Wykeham (1324–1404) helped to solve, perhaps unwittingly, when he founded his College of St. Mary of Winchester in Oxford. What chiefly concerned William was the intellectual condition of the young freshmen beginning their studies. William thought they needed better preparation, and his plan was

186

to provide a better pre-college training. Hence he planned a college where the older or senior students would take a direct part in teaching the younger students. It was a school where the student passed through all the stages of learning, beginning in childhood and continuing to the university. Wykeham was also much interested in the promotion of mutual help and charity among the scholars; he especially wished that the older members should help the younger, and this was the reason for aiding them in their studies.

Another interesting example is the College of Ave Maria at Paris University. Founded with grants of land or houses in 1336 and 1339 and additional purchases in subsequent years by John of Hubant, the college itself accommodated six "fellows" and two small boys who lived with them. The rector and governors chose the master of the college. In other colleges the master was sometimes elected. There was also a chaplain to direct the spiritual life of the students. Requirements for the fellows were that they be of legitimate birth, from good but poor families, eight or nine years of age, without notable physical defect, and able to learn. They could not remain after their sixteenth year. The founder also made provision for six poor students who lived outside the college but were supported by its six students.

Ave Maria was one of some twenty colleges established at Paris in the first half of the fourteenth century. In general their founders wanted to improve discipline and studies at Paris, and many of these colleges took in small boys, giving them preparatory training for the arts course. Enrolling boys of eight or nine, these colleges took over elementary and secondary

187

training. Some think that during the fourteenth century at Paris the age for determination was lowered to fourteen from the previously required age of twenty (1252), and so they see an additional reason why students had to be grounded in Latin at an early age.

At Ave Maria the boys were trained in grammar to their twelfth year. They began with reading, writing, and the recitation of some liturgical prayers, and studied grammar from the treatise of Donatus. Next they took up the *Doctrinale* of Alexander of Villedieu, the *Grecismus* of Everhard of Bethune (d. 1212), and the *Priscianus*. From these they passed on to the reading of various Roman poets such as Theodolus and others. Their moral education was based on readings from the Scriptures and Psalms, their daily liturgical life, the reading of the *Distichs* of Cato and good-behavior books, and the hearing of sermons. From the age of twelve to fifteen, they studied Hugocius' revered dictionary and disputed or drew up *Sophismata* in grammar, which were disputes made up of a statement followed by questions and in which one refuted the false proofs of his opponent. The library at Ave Maria had *Sophismata* in grammar and another collection in logic. Thus even into grammar school the idea of the disputation as a proof of knowledge had penetrated.

Such were some of the beginnings of the colleges at Paris and at Oxford. The growth of the English collegiate buildings, which are still in existence, did not take place till almost the end of the period with which this essay is concerned. The present buildings, at Oxford for example, belong in great part more to the period of the fifteenth to seventeenth centuries than to the Middle Ages.

188

ADDITIONAL READINGS

Gabriel, A. L., *Student Life in Ave Maria College, Mediaeval Paris*, Publications in Mediaeval Studies, The University of Notre Dame, XIV (Notre Dame, Indiana, 1955).

Haskins, C. H., "The Mediaeval Student," *The Rise of the Universities* (New York, 1923).

———, "Life of Mediaeval Students as Illustrated by their Letters," and "Manuals for Students," *Studies in Mediaeval Culture* (Oxford, 1929).

Kibre, P., "Scholarly Privileges: Their Roman Origins and Medieval Expression," *American Historical Review*, LIX (1954), 543–567.

Milburn, J. B., "University Life in Medieval Oxford," *Dublin Review*, CXXIX (1901), 72–97.

Munro, D. C., *The Mediaeval Student* (Philadelphia, 1895).

Pegues, F., "The Royal Support of Students in the 13th Century," *Speculum*, XXXI (1956), 454–462.

Rait, R. S., *Life in the Medieval University* (Cambridge, 1912).

Rashdall, H., Powicke, F. M., Emden, A. B., *The Universities of Europe in the Middle Ages* (Oxford, 1936), 3 vols.

Seybolt, R. F., *Manuale Scholarium* (Cambridge, Mass., 1921).

Thorndike, L., *University Records and Life in the Middle Ages*, University of Columbia, Records of Civilization, XXXVIII (New York, 1944).

VI. THE MEDIEVAL UNIVERSITY
IN ITS WORLD

TOWN VERSUS GOWN

The relations between students and townsmen were often none too peaceful, and some writers have emphasized the violence of students and the frequent town-versus-gown quarrels. But these town-and-gown disputes, especially during the period of the formation of the universities, had an important legal effect upon the whole structure of the university organization and upon its future development. Many of the disputes ended in securing for the university that necessary independence and protection it had to have in those days to carry on its essential work.

Paris University affords interesting examples of these quarrels. Some of the medieval critics of university students have painted a very black picture of their escapades and have described how they went about the streets armed, ready to attack the "good" town citizens, breaking into houses, quarreling among themselves, rashly rushing into conflicts which would give pause even to armed knights. Chancellor Philip at Paris described "the good old days when each master taught for himself and the name of university was unknown." Then, he said, lectures and disputations were more frequent and there was more interest in study. But now that students were united into a university, lectures and disputations were rarer and things were too hurried. He complained that the time taken from studies was spent in meetings and discussions. But the first recorded (1200) town-and-gown trouble was also the reason for the first recorded charter of privileges which the university at Paris obtained, as has been noted.[1]

These important concessions were but the first of a series of royal privileges or confirmations granted to students.[2] There was no explicit reference in the charter to the university as a corporation, however, for the king granted privileges to the scholars as scholars. The document does not deny that Paris University was a full-fledged corporation at this time; it simply does not treat the matter from a corporation viewpoint.

A much more formidable dispute, perhaps the most important in the university's history, occurred in the years 1229–1231. As in the previous quarrel thirty years before, this dispute also took its origin from a tavern squabble. Matthew of Paris in his usual colorful style has given us an interesting description of events. Some students happened to be out for a bit of a walk and on entering a tavern found some good and sweet wine there. But problems speedily arose over the size of the bill, and from words they passed "to the pulling of ears and tearing of hair." When the inn-keeper saw he was getting much the worst of it, he called on his neighbors, who rushed to his rescue, mauled the students badly and drove them out. The next day the students returned to the fray, reinforced by a goodly number of gownsmen armed with sticks and swords.

[1] Cf. documents in Norton, *Readings in the History of Education*, pp. 85, 98–99.
[2] Cf. translation, *ibid.*, pp. 94–95.

Descending on the tavern, mine host, and his neighbors, they beat them up. Then, after imbibing considerably themselves, they opened the taps of the wine kegs and sallied forth to find new fields (or taverns) to conquer. They insulted the townspeople, and soon a complaint reached the papal legate and the bishop. The latter urged the queen regent, Blanche of Castile, mother of St. Louis, to take immediate action to protect the townsmen. The queen, with "female impulsiveness," ordered out the troops, and the soldiers took revenge on a body of innocent students playing in the fields outside the town walls. It was a savage attack and several students were killed.

The masters protested vehemently to the papal legate and to the royal court, but in vain. The papal legate, not favorably disposed to the university in this case, was later recalled to Rome. Meantime, when the masters had found that their suspension of lectures did not have the desired effect, they determined upon a drastic remedy. On Monday of Easter week, April 16, 1229, they voted to close the university for a period of six years. Moreover, they took a pledge not to return even after that period unless satisfactory redress had been given to them. Soon the greater part of the university had departed from Paris. Some of them went to other schools of France, like Toulouse, Orleans, or Rheims. Many went to Angers, where they founded another university. Others crossed the channel, apparently accepting the invitation of Henry III, and there reinforced the growing universities of Oxford and Cambridge. Some chroniclers say they went also to Spain and Italy.

Pope Gregory IX (1227–1241) strove to settle the problem, and now the French royal court was seriously alarmed by the loss of the university students, who were a source of prestige and trade very important to the capital of France. By 1231 many masters were back at Paris, but they now had secured the great papal document of Gregory IX, which has been called the "Magna Carta" of the university. This document confirmed to the university by papal privilege the right of strike, which was its greatest weapon. The university corporation could strike fifteen days after due notice had been given and if no redress had been offered. They were also given authority to make statutes and to punish violation of them by exclusion from the society of masters. A further limitation was put on the chancellor by the imposition of an oath to be impartial in examinations held before him and not to reveal the votes of examining masters, and he lost his private jail, which heretofore he had used for delinquent clerics. But not all the problems between chancellor and university were solved, although the right of the chancellor at Ste. Geneviève also to grant the desired permission to teach (*licentia docendi*) to the new masters or doctors limited the power of the Paris chancellor.

All in all, from this struggle, despite its petty origins, the University of Paris gained a tremendous legal security. Because the privileges which ensued were imitated in grants to other newly founded universities during the next two centuries, this tavern quarrel had great importance.

Bologna, too, had its problems of town-and-gown, not so much with students as with professors. Professors in the Italian schools apparently tended to migrate, especially when one city was bidding against another for their services. The city fathers of Bologna decided on drastic remedies. Hearing rumors that Pilius, one of their best professors, had been approached by a delegation from Modena in order to secure his services, they

193

took immediate action. Assembling the faculty of the university, they compelled the professors to take an oath that they would teach in Bologna for the next two years. After this date (1227) down to 1312 the oath was regularly exacted by the town statutes from all who wished to teach at Bologna. Although the decree was abrogated in 1312, the penalties against doctors who absconded during the period of their contract were again put on the law books in 1334. As for Pilius, he succumbed to renewed monetary offers and fled to Modena, apparently lecturing there happily ever after.

But it was the secession not only of some professors, but of whole student groups, which troubled the Bolognese citizenry, and they legislated about that too. The city passed penalties of banishment and confiscation of goods against any scholar who dared to administer an oath to another scholar which bound him to leave the city if so commanded. This was, of course, aimed at the rectors of the universities and would have blocked the full exercise of the right of strike, or *cessatio*. The city laws obliged the universities to incorporate the town laws into their own, compelling them to swear obedience to Bologna laws. On their part the students appealed to the pope. In 1217 Pope Honorius III demanded the revocation of the law, but the city fathers refused. This caused a feud that resulted in the "banning" of the students, which meant in practice that they lost their civil rights and were liable to the confiscation of their possessions. Some time between 1217 and 1220 there occurred a dispersion of the *studium*, but a further papal remonstrance in 1220 brought the town to agree to a temporary truce. In 1222 a famous migration to Padua, and a simultaneous attempt of Emperor Frederick II to wreck the university as well as the

194

Lombard league, brought the city fathers to agree to give up their struggle to limit the power of the rectors of the universities. As late as 1432, however, there was a city statute decreeing the death penalty against anyone who entered into a conspiracy to transfer the university, and the same punishment was enacted against any professor *more than fifty years of age* who dared to leave Bologna for the purpose of lecturing elsewhere. If the offending professor were under fifty, the fine was two hundred ducats—a large sum in those days.

As decades passed, the students gained more privileges: the civil rights of the town (but almost never *political* rights), the right to will or inherit property, to give evidence in court; and measures were taken to protect their property.

Another dispute between citizens and students at Bologna made clear the power of the university. One of the scholars, attempting to abduct the daughter of a town notary, had been aided by some fellow students. He was caught and executed. In reply the majority of students and many professors seceded to Siena. It took a year for the reconciliation to be worked out, and the city compelled its mayor (*podestà*) to take a public disciplining in the Dominican church, and then built a commemorative chapel for the university which was afterwards known as St. Mary's of the Peace (*Santa Maria della Pace*).

Oxford in its early history much resembles Paris in its acquisition of privileges from town-and-gown riots. The first recorded disputes date back to 1209, when two or three scholars were hanged as a result of a pitched battle between townsmen and gownsmen originating in the killing (accidental, the chronicler says) of a townswoman by a university student.

195

At any rate, there was the usual dispersion of students and masters to safer parts, and the university at Oxford came to a stop for some time. A document of the papal legate in England in 1214 forms the basis for the development of the privileges which the university garnered through the centuries. The provisions in this 1214 solution required the townsmen who had taken part in the hanging of the clerks to do penance in a barefoot procession to the graves of their victims and then to the cemetery for their proper burial. (Since, owing to a controversy between King John and Pope Innocent III, England had been under an interdict [1208–1214], ecclesiastical burial had been impossible at the time of the execution.)

There were other provisions much more practical for the students; namely, for ten years one-half the rent of the residences occupied by the students was to be remitted, and for ten more years these rents were to remain at the ceiling fixed by joint authority of town and university. Food was to be sold at a reasonable rate, and fifty townsmen swore that these provisions would be kept. Any clerk arrested by town officials had henceforth to be turned over to the bishop or chancellor or someone delegated by the bishop. Several other incidents of this type occurred at Oxford during the thirteenth and fourteenth centuries, and from each of them there usually resulted either a confirmation or an extension of university privileges.

The same kind of problems arose in other university centers. As has been noted, chroniclers mention the fact that a considerable group from the university of Bologna transferred to Padua in the year 1222; and next the masters and students, after being situated there for some six years, made an agreement with the city fathers of Vercelli to transfer their *studium* to that city, for already the Paduans had not measured up to their expectations. Although the university at Padua declined after the movement to Vercelli, it revived and continued on its educational way in 1260, owing to a change in local politics and another exodus of students from Bologna, caused this time by the war between Bologna and Forlì. Florence attempted to lure away discontented professors and students from Bologna with bribes in 1321, but without much success. Florence enacted stringent laws making study at its own university obligatory, and by the end of the fifteenth century it had a flourishing university.

These troubles between town and gown at Paris and Oxford were often similar in origin. Friction between merchants of food or liquor stores near the campus and university students were often the occasion of the quarreling. In northern Italy, with its more lively urban life, and with city vying with city for the leadership in commerce, art, and literature, it was no wonder that competition for the possession of a *studium generale* or university was so frequent a cause of dispute. Their methods remind one of modern talent scouts and their managers. The reader, upon investigation of the sources, will find that the comparison is apt even with regard to minor details like living accommodations. The penalties for violation of contract were much more drastic in those days, but that such legislation was effective seems doubtful, for there were several secessions from Bologna despite the drastic town statutes there.

The legal privileges involved make these medieval town-and-gown disputes more important than disturbances between the students and local police in a university city today. The privileges obtained as a result of some of these petty struggles established the various centers of learning on a solid and inde-

197

pendent basis at a time in history when, unless they had secured this independence, they might well have disappeared. For, after all, the universities were generally poor; they had neither large school buildings nor landed endowments of their own, and they were composed in great part of a group of "foreigners" who were neither rich nor influential. Indeed, so important to the future of university education were some one or two of the tavern brawls—those at Paris, for example—that one might almost be persuaded that the medieval university did indeed "live off its misfortunes."

THE FAVORITE OF THE POPES

When it comes to the actual foundation of the universities, the list of 79 universities founded in medieval Europe before 1500 as given in Rashdall's classic work gives some 53 as founded immediately, or not long afterwards confirmed, by a papal university document. In 1233 when Gregory IX founded the University of Toulouse he declared that any graduate master of Toulouse was entitled to teach in any of the other *studia* without further examination. This was the *jus ubique docendi*, the right of teaching anywhere, i.e. in any other *studia*. The desirability of having such a privilege grew to such an extent that even universities like Bologna and Paris, founded long before, were formally given this right—Bologna in 1291 and Paris in 1292, both by Nicholas IV. Oxford, which had been recognized as a university for so many decades, was given the title of *studia ex consuetudine* by the Italian jurists when they came to line up the legal distinctions regarding the various universities.

A further, and in the beginning probably the primary, privilege conferred by the papal document was the right granted to clerics or ecclesiastical officials who had a benefice to go to the university to study and at the same time to keep receiving the revenues from their benefice. (A benefice was an ecclesiastical office carrying with it some revenue.) Of course such beneficed clerics would have to provide a subordinate, paying him a percentage of the total revenues, but they were free to study and at the same time had enough to support themselves.

These two privileges help to explain the close relationship between the universities and the popes. But it should always be remembered that the students of a university were mostly all *clerics* (in some degree), and by that very fact the university as a group came directly under the jurisdiction of the Church.

The University of Toulouse is an interesting example of the way in which a university was founded. Indeed, some have seen in the University of Toulouse *the* example, which created the precedent of actually "founding" corporations of learning after the Parisian model in various parts of Europe. Whether or not it originated the practice, the example of the founding of Toulouse University, and the actual documents with which it was legalized, had a profound effect upon the founding of other universities by the various popes. The basic idea and purpose of creating Toulouse University was to provide an intellectual antidote to Albigensianism.

Apart from the immediate purpose which occasioned the

199

foundation of the university, the documents and the organizational framework given it have an interest all their own. In the treaty which ended the war between Raymond Count of Toulouse and Louis IX of France, one section had to do with the foundation of this university. Raymond was to pay salaries for about fourteen professors: four masters in theology, two in canon law, six in arts, and two in grammar; the theologians got fifty marks a year and the grammarians ten. A very florid announcement (some do not believe it was actually circulated) was written containing a glowing description of the new institution, and definitely worded to attract students from Paris. One of the peculiarities of Toulouse was that it was to be set up with all four faculties. But it should also be added that Toulouse had hard going for many years.

The constitution of Toulouse University was an attempt at a *via media* between the Parisian master-dominated guild and the student "universities" of Bologna. But preference was given to the Parisian model, and student control was only in evidence (and then not very much) in the jurist faculty. The interest in the university lies rather in the fact that it forms an example of an institution set up and equipped immediately with a legal existence, and not gradually developing as did Oxford or Paris or Bologna.[3] As such it set a happy precedent for the creation of more of these intellectual guilds for learning in cities not previously favored. The importance to European civilization of the actualization of this idea can hardly be exaggerated, for from that day to this the practice has continued in Europe and the Americas, and then in other parts of the world, of founding universities. There has been achieved a continuity in

[3] Cf. document in Thorndike, *Univ. Records*, pp. 32–35.

the educational development of European civilization not to be found in the other civilizations. This general practice, then, of pope—and, to a lesser extent, of emperor or king—of setting up these intellectual guilds and endowing them with legal existence, jurisdictions, and privileges became routine procedure. As a result, the major number of medieval universities trace their existence to papal grants of confirmation.

From the thirteenth to the fifteenth century papal policy consistently protected the universities. In the case of Paris University on several occasions papal support saved the day against the opposition of the local ecclesiastical officials—for instance, in 1215, and especially by the great Magna Carta of Paris given by Gregory IX in 1231. But the end of the Middle Ages witnessed the growing power of the monarchies, and this tended to bring an end to some of the universities' most cherished liberties. In 1499 the University of Paris lost its great weapon of *cessatio*. For some this has seemed no great loss, but rather the passing away of one of "those privileged licenses and uncouth, lawless liberties which so strangely tempered the iron regime of medieval feudalism." However, the rise of modern totalitarianism and the danger of absolute government control of education has modified modern viewpoints in this matter.

If the pope happened to be a former student, the university was even more certain of papal protection. This happened at Orleans in 1306, when the university, then in its infancy, came into serious conflict with the bishop. After appeal to Rome, a series of bulls were issued by Clement V (1305–1314), formerly an Orleans student, giving to the university the same administrative set-up and privileges that Toulouse had—i.e.,

201

the right to make laws for certain purposes, the right of electing their rector, and so on. In general, although the universities had some severe critics among the papal reformers as regards their student-celebrations, their most consistent and greatest protector was the Pope of Rome. He it was who granted, increased, and protected their privileged status in a world of often-conflicting jurisdictions.

One of the perennial problems of any system of education is the question of who pays the bills. The student in the medieval educational world had problems with tuition, living costs, and books, just as does his modern successor. There was at hand, however, a system of subsidization which aided the medieval student greatly, but which has long since passed away. Since medieval students were nearly all clerics, they enjoyed the legal privileges and exemptions accorded to the student by both ecclesiastical and civil governments. Although many of them did not even take minor orders, they were considered clerics in a sense sufficient to share in the privileges of the clerical state. Now a common form of ecclesiastical financial support in the Middle Ages was the benefice system, by means of which the revenues from some ecclesiastical parish or possession were assigned to a cleric as his main salary for subsistence; and one of the most important privileges conferred on a new university by the papal document of foundation was the right, which we have already noted, for beneficed ecclesiastics to come to that university to study, and still to draw their benefice pay. From such beginnings as this grew the papal provision system as far as it was related to the universities. Canonical tendencies of ecclesiastical centralization during the thirteenth and fourteenth centuries meant in effect that the Roman Curia increased the number of benefices to which *it* could appoint benefice-holders. With the moving of the popes to Avignon during the period 1309–1378, Europe saw the development of that great financial administrative system which was probably the best example of its type Europe had yet seen, but which brought in its train all the evils of a centralized bureaucracy. Still, there were definite advantages to the system, and the universities were certainly the beneficiaries.

The papal policy of appointing to benefices always took into account the scholarly qualifications of the applicants, which meant in practice that the university students and graduates were favored over the non-university ecclesiastics. Thus from the university point of view, the papal provision system was apt to be a much more kindly dispenser of benefices than were the local bishops, presumably not so much interested in scholarly qualifications. The papal provision system was clearly regulated, and the university graduate was favored over the cleric who had no such training. When the Great Schism (1378–1417) occurred and the power of appointing to benefices was placed in the hands of the French bishops rather than the Roman Curia, the outcry of the university was immediate and loud. The reason was obvious. The universities had been the favorites of the popes, and the papal provision system had consistently given preference to the university graduate over his non-university competitor.

The importance of this consistent papal policy, lasting through several centuries, of showing favor to those ecclesiastics who had university training is evident. Long before any group of organizations, or before any national government, set itself to subsidize to any great extent the university student body, the popes and the Roman Curia developed and consistently pursued a policy of financing university education on an international scale.

SECULAR MASTERS VERSUS FRIAR PROFESSORS

The historian of today attempting to understand the relations of the religious orders and the secular masters at the universities feels somewhat in the position of a person trying to comprehend a family quarrel. The medieval world has passed away. The medieval universities have changed into the modern, with a different environment and very different problems. Perhaps a modern analogy might be of help. No one connected with universities in America today can be unaware that there are serious differences of opinion between those who are considered the "faculty" of a university and those who are called its "administrators." Sometimes there is not a little friction and useless duplication of effort through lack of understanding and communication. But no serious historian would so picture individual instances of infrequent occurrence that his readers would think that daily life at a university consisted of pitched battles between administration and faculty, to the exclusion of such mundane things as classes. Unfortunately, sometimes the disputes between the members of the new religious orders, mainly Dominicans and Franciscans, and the secular masters has been given undue emphasis. There were strained relations between seculars and religious—for instance, at Paris in 1229, and again in 1252–1256. But in the history of a university

204

through several centuries of vigorous life, such incidents were relatively infrequent.

One must recall the type of intellectual training which Dominican students as members of their order received, and remember that in general the other orders of friars (Franciscan, Austin, Carmelite) had patterned their study life after the Dominican model. St. Dominic had founded his order to provide educated preachers against the heresy of Albigensianism and against that perennial danger to religion—ignorance. There developed in his order a comprehensive educational system paralleling the university training in many of its details. As early as 1228 we have legislation in the Dominican order providing a conventual school and a lecturer who must have studied theology for at least four years. The text in the conventual school, which also took in some non-Dominican students, was the Bible and the *Sentences* of Peter Lombard. Then there were special schools established for each province of the order, and finally *studia generalia* to which students could be sent from various provinces. In a certain sense the whole order was a kind of university. Besides, the establishment of the *studia generalia* in university towns was an aid to gaining novices from among the university students. A *studium generale* of the order had been established in Paris as early as 1228.

Furthermore, the philosophical studies preparatory to theology were made in these schools of the order, for the religious-order students did not attend the college of arts at the university and did not take a master's degree in arts. Here was a basic cause of the friction between the secular masters and the religious-order theologians: the insistence of the latter upon the

205

right to proceed to theology without having studied in the arts school or taught as regents in arts, and on the other hand the exclusive attitude of the secular masters (see above, page 135).

When the famous quarrel broke out between townspeople and students and the University of Paris decreed a *cessatio* in 1229, the Dominicans continued teaching in their school and apparently opened their doors to externs who wished to continue their studies during the strike. In other words, the Dominicans did not follow the magisterial "union" in this matter but continued to conduct their own theological school. One can easily understand how there were two sides to the question. But when the dispute was settled and students and masters took up their disputations at the old stands, the position of the friars does not seem to have been questioned. Matters were further complicated by the entrance into the Dominicans of John St. Giles and into the Franciscans of Alexander of Hales, both of whom were well-known masters. As a result there were now two doctors lecturing in theology at the Dominican convent of St. Jacques, but apparently nobody at this time complained of illegality.

Then in the 1250's there was a definite effort by the secular masters to limit the number of masters belonging to religious orders and teaching in the order schools. Besides, two Dominicans and one Franciscan refused to obey the *cessatio* order in 1253 arising out of another town-and-gown dispute. The recalcitrant masters were expelled from the theological faculty, and both sides appealed to Rome. There was considerable pamphleteering, and one of the seculars, Master William of St. Amour, wrote a broadside against the whole concept of the religious life of the friars. This in turn called forth the efforts of the greatest scholars on the mendicant side, namely, St. Thomas Aquinas and St. Bonaventure, who answered him at length, thus providing modern readers with excellent treatises explaining the theory of monasticism as interpreted by the mendicant orders.

Pope Alexander IV directed the readmission of the mendicants to the society of masters under pain of excommunication. The secular masters still refused to obey, and in turn forbade university students to attend the mendicant schools. When the university beadles attempted to publish the bann in the schools of the mendicants, they not unnaturally met with a warm reception. On the other hand, friars soon found that venturing forth from their houses of study was a serious business, which not only exposed them to ridicule but made them preferred targets for garbage poured out of upstairs windows! When peace was restored, the mendicants maintained in general their former status, but feelings were strained for several years thereafter.

Some writers have laid stress on the constitutional side of this dispute and found in the various legal aspects of the problems the cause of much of the controversy. In addition, however, there were human factors which help to explain the situation. As can be detected from some of the chroniclers, such as Richer and Thomas of Cantimpré, an evident cause lay in the popularity of the mendicant teachers and the fact that there were not enough theological students to go around. Another reason, already noted, was the claim of the religious-order students to enter on their theological doctorate without actually taking the classes of the secular masters in the arts. They were, of course, trained in their own schools, but this did not

207

make their procedure any more palatable to the seculars. In fact, the faculty of arts at Paris explicitly refused to admit them.

The popularity of the mendicant masters and the fact that the friars' schools were a parallel organization to the schools of the secular masters helps us to understand the friction between the groups. It is not necessary, as one chronicler does, to trace it to the "inferior teaching" of the secular masters, which he further explains as due to the heavy eating, excessive vacations, and long sleeps of the secular masters in contrast to the mendicants, who stayed up late and studied!

There were other aspects to the dispute arising from the discussions about the wide powers of preaching and hearing confessions granted by the popes to the mendicant orders. Much petty jealousy found its way into the literature of the times, and sometimes such matter is quoted as serious history by later writers.

THE INFLUENCE OF THE MEDIEVAL UNIVERSITY

It is no easy task to evaluate the influence of the medieval universities because medieval statistics are few and far between. The first thing to find out is how many people went to the university. This immediately raises difficulties; for instance, the jurist Odofredus wrote (about 1250) that in 1220 there had been 10,000 students at Bologna. Wyclif claims 60,000 scholars for Oxford many years before his time, although while he taught there, he said there were less than 3,000. Rabbanus Gauma, Nestorian monk, said that there were 30,000 at Paris in 1287. To modern scholarship these high figures are mentally indigestible. It has been noted that generally whenever the estimate is for conditions as the observer himself knew them, that estimate is far less than the numbers which he assigns for the period before his time. There is the additional fact that the medieval chronicler liked nice round figures. Witness the numbers assigned to some of the crusading hosts, in comparison with the actual contract signed with Venice to transport the bulk of the Fourth Crusade—4,500 knights and 20,000 foot-soldiers, of whom not more than about 1,000 knights seem to have come to Venice to be transported.

Modern authors generally estimate the enrollment of the medieval university at Oxford at somewhere between 1,500 and 2,000 with the highest at 3,000; for Paris, 5,000 to 7,000 would probably be representative. The special difficulty of the Parisian figures as given by contemporaries is that the contemporary was frequently using the figure as an argument rather than an estimate. A modern scholar's estimates on some of the German universities are as follows.[4]

Leipzig	504
Erfurt	427
Wittenberg	420
Köln	388
Ingolstadt	296
Rostock	222
Heidelberg	219
Tübingen	161
Freiburg	147
Greifswald	84

[4] Eulenberg, quoted in H. Rashdall, *The Universities of Europe in the Middle Ages* (Oxford, 1936), III, p. 334.

These figures give one scholar's estimate of average yearly attendance down to 1540; the difficulty with them is that they also include the period immediately after the religious revolutions and reformations had begun (1520–1540), and the universities were hard hit during these years. The same writer has also concluded that the average German university student did not stay at the university for more than about a year and nine months and that the majority took no degree. About two-fifths received their bachelor's degree and perhaps one-twentieth studied in the higher faculties.

Nevertheless when the various indications are all put together and compared with the population of the medieval world, as our scanty records indicate it, the results show a *comparatively* high percentage of people engaged in university work. From the viewpoint of numbers, as indicating influence on the cultures of the time, the medieval university compares favorably with modern times, and certainly with the comparative student population figures for the United States in the 1800's to the 1850's, for example.

The papal provision system referred to above was another indication of the influence of the universities on the opinion of those appointing to benefices and administrative offices. The number of bishops in various sees of Europe during this period who were graduates of the universities was high. But what is perhaps more astonishing is the value that was put upon university training by kings and princes, by bishops and popes, in seeking their subordinate officials. Kings often found their advisors and diplomats in the universities, and not always in the law faculties either, although the importance of that faculty in the conduct of the governmental business of medieval Europe was very great. Some have said that the medieval education was too practical, that it taught men "to work rather than to enjoy." Whether this be true or not, the medieval university graduate had many career possibilities before him.

Another way to gauge the influence of medieval universities is to note the part which their graduates played in their world. One group were the popes from the thirteenth to fifteenth centuries. Their educational backgrounds are interesting examples.

Innocent III (1198–1216) was a graduate of Paris and Bologna universities and an outstanding jurist. Honorius III (1216–1227) had been a tutor of Emperor Frederick II and was a patron of both Paris and Bologna. Gregory IX (1227–1241) was educated at Paris and Bologna. Innocent IV (1243–1254) was a former professor of canon law at Bologna. Alexander IV (1254–1261) was educated at Anagni, and Urban IV (1261–1264) took his doctorate from the University of Paris. Clement IV (1265–1268) had been a jurist in the service of the French king after finishing his law studies at Paris, and Innocent V (1276), who received his doctorate in theology from Paris in 1259, had been a professor of theology. John XXI (1276–1277) was also known as Peter of Spain, the writer of a famous textbook in logic. He had studied at Paris under Albert the Great and John of Parma, working in both theology and medicine. He was a former professor of medicine at Siena University. Boniface VIII (1294–1303), a famous canon lawyer, had studied at Spoleto and possibly at Paris. Benedict XI (1303–1304) was a Dominican professor of theology and a former master-general of his order. Clement V (1305–1314) had studied arts at Toulouse and canon and civil law at Orleans and Bologna, John XXII (1316–1334) studied theology and law at Montpellier and Paris and was professor of canon and civil law at the universities of Toulouse and Cahors. Benedict XII (1334–1342) was a doctor of theology from Paris. Clement VI (1342–1352) was a former professor at Paris. Innocent VI (1352–1362) was a former professor of civil law at Toulouse. Urban V (1362–1370) had studied theology and canon law at Toulouse, Montpellier, Paris, and Avignon. He was a former professor of canon law at Montpellier and had taught at Toulouse, Avignon, and Paris. Gregory XI (1370–1378) was a graduate of the university of Perugia. Benedict XIII (1394–d. 1422[?], Avignon Line), better known, perhaps, as Pedro de Luna, had been a professor of law at Montpellier. Innocent VII (1404–1406) was a former professor of jurisprudence at Perugia and Padua.

Probably the most popular medieval graduate degree was law, either canon or civil or both. The number of the popes during the period listed above who were lawyers is noteworthy. Canon law was a study which fitted one for an ecclesiastical career. The theologians, on the other hand, were fewer, and seemingly did not rise so quickly in the administrative world.

Another advantage which the medieval university could employ to extend its influence was the internationality of its student body. This student body was usually a mixture of nationalities. Among her top-ranking scholastic theologians and philosophers in the thirteenth century, Paris numbered Albert the Great, Thomas Aquinas, Duns Scotus, and Bonaventure. None of them were Frenchmen. A study of the rolls of Bologna University finds more than fifty English scholars there during the 1400's taking their doctorate in law, and many of them rising to high administrative posts in civil or ecclesiastical service. It was only with the increasing development of nationalism that the cosmopolitan student culture began to wane, and the bitterness between the nationalities at fifteenth-century Prague was but a sad foretaste of the future.

The political influence of the universities as individual bodies was a strong one. Paris, of course, was the outstanding example. She did not hesitate to take the title of "the eldest daughter of the King of France," and at times she was an outspoken one. Several times Paris University was called upon to mediate between the Court and some quarreling faction within the kingdom; for instance, during the rebellions of 1357–1358 under Etienne Marcel, or again during the latter part of the Hundred Years' War when France was torn by civil discord. An even more impressive example was the role which the university played in attempting to solve the electoral problem which brought on the Great Western Schism.

A characteristic of medieval university training which helps to explain the influence of the universities was the emphasis that all knowledge, whether it be in arts, medicine, law, or theology, be an *articulate* science. The medieval graduate had to be able to express himself, to argue, discuss, and debate.

EPILOGUE

The first debt which the modern university owes to its medieval predecessor is one of existence. Great as were the other civilizations of the past, none of them produced universities as we understand the term today. There is nothing like the continuity of preserving, teaching, and finding knowledge that is the glorious history of the medieval universities. Their primary contribution is *themselves*. Although we have changed some of the methods, added new studies, and multiplied buildings, resources, and faculties, basically the essential idea of the medieval university as a place where an apprentice to learning could become a master of it has remained the same. Our modern universities are perhaps our most medieval organizations.

A second evident debt is the creation of the modern American and European professional man. That our doctors, lawyers, and professors should be *university*-trained is something which the great pagan civilizations never achieved. The professional standards, the unique position of the European or American doctor, lawyer, or university professor as a cultured specialist possessing a common heritage of European civilization is most important. In preserving what is best in our civilization against another way of life, it may be that this common institution which transcends nationality may in the long run protect more securely than armed forces.

ADDITIONAL READINGS

Dibben, L. B., "Secretaries in the 13th and 14th Centuries," *English Historical Review*, XXV (1910), 430–444.

Gabriel, A. L., *Student Life in Ave Maria College, Mediaeval Paris*, Publications in Mediaeval Studies, The University of Notre Dame, XIV (Notre Dame, Indiana, 1955).

Gray, A., "The Beginnings of Colleges," *History*, VI (1921), 1–10.

Gross, C., "The Political Influence of the University of Paris in the Middle Ages," *American Historical Review*, VI (1901), 440–445.

Haskins, G. L., "The University of Oxford and the *Jus Ubique Docendi*," *English Historical Review*, LVI (1941), 281–292.

Little, A. G., *Franciscan Papers, Lists and Documents* (Manchester University Press, 1943).

——, *Grey Friars at Oxford* (Oxford, 1892).

Powicke, F. M., "Some Problems in the History of the Medieval University," *Transactions of the Royal Historical Society*, XXI (1934), 1–18.

Rashdall, H., Powicke, F. M., Emden, A. B., *The Universities of Europe in the Middle Ages* (Oxford, 1936), 3 vols.

Smith, Cyril E., *The University of Toulouse in the Middle Ages* (Milwaukee, 1958).

215

APPENDIX: DOCUMENTS

THE EDUCATION OF
JOHN OF SALISBURY

Metalogicon, ed. Webb, 1929, lib. II, cap.
10; Migne, *Patrologia latina*, vol. 199, cols.
867–69.

When first as a mere lad I went to Gaul for an education in the
year after the illustrious king of the Angles, Henry, the lion of
justice, departed from human affairs, I betook me to the Peripatetic
of Palais[2] who at that time presided on the hill of Sainte Geneviève
as a doctor celebrated and admired by all. There at his feet I received the first rudiments of the art of logic and as far as my small
talents permitted I received with all the avidity of my mind whatever fell from his lips. Then after his departure, which seemed to
me all too soon, I attached myself to master Alberic, who shone
forth as the dialectian most esteemed among the rest and was indeed the sharpest opponent of the nominalists. Thus, spending
almost the whole of two years on the hill, I had as my teachers in
this art Alberic and master Robert of Melun—to use the name

---

[1] Reprinted with permission from Lynn Thorndike, *University
Records and Life in the Middle Ages* (New York: Columbia University
Press, 1944), pp. 11–14.
[2] Abelard is meant.

that he earned in the school system, although he was of English birth. One of them, very exact in everything, found room for questioning everywhere, so that no matter how polished the surface he could find some flaw in it and, as they say, a rush would not have been without knots for him, for even in it he would have shown where there ought to be knots! The other, on the other hand, very quick in his answers, never dodged any question by means of subterfuges, nay he would take either side of a contradiction, or by bringing out the manifold arguments he would teach that there was no one answer. So one was subtle and prolific in questions; the other, clear-headed, brief, and apt in his answers. If the qualities of these two had all been combined in any one man, his equal as a disputant would not have been found in our age. For both were sharp-witted and hard students and in my opinion [would have become great and famous men in physical studies, if they had built on the great foundation of literature, if they had devoted as much attention to the remains of the ancients as they gave applause to their own inventions.] So much for the time in which I heard them. For afterwards one of them going to Bologna unlearned what he used to teach and on his return untaught it— whether for the better, let those judge who heard him both before and after. The other forsooth becoming proficient in divine letters won the glory of an even higher philosophy and of a more celebrated name. Drilled by them for all of two years, I became so accustomed to allotting places, and to rules, and to the other elementary rudiments with which the minds of boys are instructed and in which the aforesaid doctors were most capable and expeditious, that it seemed to me that I knew all these things as well as my own nails and fingers. Evidently I had learned this: to account my knowledge with youthful levity as of more importance than it was. I thought myself an adept because I was quick in those things that I had heard.

Then coming to myself and measuring my powers, thanks to the kindness of my teachers I straightway betook me to the grammarian of Conches and heard him lecture for three years. Meanwhile I did a great deal of reading, nor shall I ever regret that time. Later on I followed Richard Bishop, a man ignorant of scarcely any science, who had more heart than mouth, more learning than facility, truth than vanity, virtue than ostentation; and what I had heard from others received all again from him and I learned some things which I had not heard pertaining to the quadrivium, on which to some extent I had previously heard Hardewin the Teuton. I reviewed rhetoric too, which before I had understood little of, when with some others I heard it scantily discussed by master Theodoric. But later I received it more fully from Peter Helias. And inasmuch as I had become the tutor of some nobles' children, who supplied me with a livelihood, destitute as I was of aid from friends and relatives, God relieving my poverty, I was stimulated by the requirements of my position and the urging of the boys to recall more frequently to mind what I had heard. Wherefore I struck up a closer friendship with master Adam, a man of keenest wit and, whatever others may think, of much learning, who applied himself to Aristotle more than the rest. So that, although he was not my master, he kindly gave me the benefit of his learning and showed himself very open with me, which he did to no one else or to very few. For he was thought to be of a jealous disposition.

Meanwhile William of Soissons—who later made an engine to lay siege, as his adherents say, to old-fashioned logic and reach unexpected consequences and destroy the opinions of the ancients —was teaching the first elements of logic, and finally I added him to the preceptor already mentioned. There perhaps he learned that the same is from contradiction, when Aristotle is maligned, because the same when it is and when it is not is not necessarily the same. And also when something is, it is not necessary that it be the same and not be. For nothing comes from contradiction, and it is impossible that contradiction come from anything. Wherefore I could not be induced by the impelling engine of my friend to believe that all impossibles come from one impossible. From this I was withdrawn by the scantiness of my income, the request of my associates, and the advice of friends, to assume the position of a teacher. I obeyed.

Returning at the end of three years I found master Gilbert and heard him lecture on logic and theology, but all too soon he was removed. Robert Pullus succeeded, praiseworthy alike in life and learning. Then Simon of Poissy received me, a conscientious lecturer but dull disputant. But I had these two teachers in theology exclusively. Thus well nigh twelve years slipped by, as I was occupied with varied studies.

So I thought it would be pleasant to revisit the old classmates whom I had left and whom dialectic still detained on the Mount, to confer with them concerning the old problems, and, by comparing notes, measure our respective progress. I found the same men and just where they were, for they neither seemed to have advanced an inch towards solving the old problems, nor had they added a single new one. As teachers they drove with the same goads that drove them as students. In only one respect had they grown proficient: they had unlearned moderation, they knew no modesty, to such a degree that one despaired of their reformation. Thus I learned by experience an evident lesson, that just as dialectic facilitates other disciplines, so, if studied alone, it remains lifeless and sterile, nor does it stimulate the soul to bear fruits of Philosophy, unless it conceives elsewhere.

DOCUMENT 2[1]

RULES OF THE UNIVERSITY
OF PARIS, 1215

Chartularium universitatis Parisiensis, I,
78–79.

Robert, cardinal legate, prescribes the mode of lecturing in arts and
in theology, indicates what books the masters of arts should not
read, formulates the discipline of the scholars and the state of the
university generally.

Robert, servant of the cross of Christ by divine pity cardinal
priest of the title, St. Stephen in Mons Caelius, legate of the apostolic see, to all the masters and scholars of Paris eternal greetings in the
Lord. Let all know that, since we have had a special mandate from
the pope to take effective measures to reform the state of the
Parisian scholars for the better, wishing with the counsel of good
men to provide for the tranquillity of the scholars in the future,
we have decreed and ordained in this wise:

No one shall lecture in the arts at Paris before he is twenty-one
years of age, and he shall have heard lectures for at least six years
before he begins to lecture, and he shall promise to lecture for at
least two years, unless a reasonable cause prevents, which he ought

[1] Reprinted with permission from Lynn Thorndike, *University
Records and Life in the Middle Ages* (New York: Columbia University
Press, 1944), pp. 27–30.

223

to prove publicly or before examiners. He shall not be stained by any infamy, and when he is ready to lecture, he shall be examined according to the form which is contained in the writing of the lord bishop of Paris, where is contained the peace confirmed between the chancellor and scholars by judges delegated by the pope, namely, by the bishop and dean of Troyes and by P. the bishop and J. the chancellor of Paris approved and confirmed. And they shall lecture on the books of Aristotle on dialectic old and new in the schools ordinarily and not *ad cursum*. They shall also lecture on both Priscians ordinarily, or at least on one. They shall not lecture on feast days except on philosophers and rhetoric and the quadrivium and *Barbarismus* and ethics, if it please them, and the fourth book of the *Topics*. They shall not lecture on the books of Aristotle on metaphysics and natural philosophy or on summaries of them or concerning the doctrine of master David of Dinant or the heretic Amaury or Mauritius of Spain.

In the *principia* and meetings of the masters and in the responsions or oppositions of the boys and youths there shall be no drinking. They may summon some friends or associates, but only a few. Donations of clothing or other things as has been customary, or more, we urge should be made, especially to the poor. None of the masters lecturing in arts shall have a cope except one round, black and reaching to the ankles, at least while it is new. Use of the pallium is permitted. No one shall wear with the round cope shoes that are ornamented or with elongated pointed toes. If any scholar in arts or theology dies, half of the masters of arts shall attend the funeral at one time, the other half the next time, and no one shall leave until the sepulture is finished, unless he has reasonable cause. If any master in arts or theology dies, all the masters shall keep vigils, each shall read or cause to be read the Psalter, each shall attend the church where is celebrated the watch until midnight or the greater part of the night, unless reasonable cause prevent. On the day when the master is buried, no one shall lecture or dispute.

We fully confirm to them the meadow of St. Germain in that condition in which it was adjudicated to them.

Each master shall have jurisdiction over his scholar. No one shall occupy a classroom or house without asking the consent of the tenant, provided one has a chance to ask it. No one shall receive the licentiate from the chancellor or another for money given or promise made or other condition agreed upon. Also, the masters and scholars can make both between themselves and with other persons obligations and constitutions supported by faith or penalty or oath in these cases: namely, the murder or mutilation of a scholar or atrocious injury done a scholar, if justice should not be forthcoming, arranging the prices of lodgings, costume, burial, lectures and disputations, so, however, that the university be not thereby dissolved or destroyed.

As to the status of the theologians, we decree that no one shall lecture at Paris before his thirty-fifth year and unless he has studied for eight years at least, and has heard the books faithfully and in classrooms, and has attended lectures in theology for five years before he gives lectures himself publicly. And none of these shall lecture before the third hour on days when masters lecture. No one shall be admitted at Paris to formal lectures or to preachings unless he shall be of approved life and science. No one shall be a scholar at Paris who has no definite master.

Moreover, that these decrees may be observed inviolate, we by virtue of our legatine authority have bound by the knot of excommunication all who shall contumaciously presume to go against these our statutes, unless within fifteen days after the offense they have taken care to emend their presumption before the university of masters and scholars or other persons constituted by the university. Done in the year of Grace 1215, the month of August.

Document 3[1]

OFFICE OF UNIVERSITY BEDELL, PARIS

Chartularium universitatis Parisiensis, I, 418.

These are the statutes which the bedells of the university of Paris obligate themselves faithfully to observe, giving personal security. They ought to attend the opening lecture of each person incepting, poor or otherwise, from beginning to end, unless it is well known that they have been sent by the person incepting or the proctor of his nation on some special errand or for some special common examination of the nation, or unless they have to attend funeral obsequies, or unless their own bodily infirmity prevents them, or unless they are detained by some other legitimate and notorious occasion, if there can be any other than those specified. If, however, they absent themselves unexcused by any of the said occasions, they ought to forfeit their portion of that purse which he gives who incepts, which portion, I say, should go to the proctor of the said bedell who forfeits it. Also, if it is enjoined upon any bedell to call a meeting either special or general, and it can be proved by three or four masters that he has not cited them, he should know that he will similarly forfeit a portion of each purse, two solidi, which portion likewise will go to the proctor of that nation.

[1] Reprinted with permission from Lynn Thorndike, *University Records and Life in the Middle Ages* (New York: Columbia University Press, 1944), pp. 72–73.

Also, if he ought to announce a course and it can be proved that he has failed to go to all classes, he should know that he will incur the same penalty and same loss in the same manner as aforesaid. Also, each bedell ought early in the morning on each day to visit the classes not only of the rector or his own proctor but also of every proctor of every nation, which if he does not do, let him know that he will incur the same loss in the same manner. Also, if he shall fail to attend the common examination of anyone of his nation or shall be proved to have betrayed the university's secrets, let him know that he shall forfeit one purse as has been said. Also, if he is absent on Friday at the vespers of his nation, he shall lose two pence and for mass two. Also, if he does not have a calendar and is deficient in announcing to individuals a Feast which is not well known, or even in not preventing disputation when he should, for each such offense he shall forfeit four pence, all which pence the proctor of the nation of the delinquent bedell should keep for the use of his nation.

DOCUMENT 4[1]

COURSES IN ARTS, PARIS, 1255

Chartularium universitatis Parisiensis, I,
277–79.

In the year of the Lord 1254. Let all know that we, all and each, masters of arts by our common assent, no one contradicting, because of the new and incalculable peril which threatens in our faculty—some masters hurrying to finish their lectures sooner than the length and difficulty of the texts permits, for which reason both masters in lecturing and scholars in hearing make less progress —worrying over the ruin of our faculty and wishing to provide for our status, have decreed and ordained for the common utility and the reparation of our university to the honor of God and the church universal that all and single masters of our faculty in the future shall be required to finish the texts which they shall have begun on the feast of St. Remy at the times below noted, not before.

The Old Logic, namely the book of Porphyry, the *Praedicamenta, Periarmeniae, Divisions* and *Topics* of Boethius, except the fourth, on the feast of the Annunciation of the blessed Virgin or the last day for lectures preceding. *Priscian minor* and *major*,

[1] Reprinted with permission from Lynn Thorndike, *University Records and Life in the Middle Ages* (New York: Columbia University Press, 1944), pp. 64–66.

Topics and *Elenchi*, *Prior* and *Posterior Analytics* they must finish
in the said or equal time. The *Ethics* through four books in twelve
weeks, if they are read with another text, if *per se*, not with another,
in half that time. Three short texts, namely *Sex principia*, *Barbarismus*, Priscian on accent, if read together and nothing else
with them, in six weeks. The *Physics* of Aristotle, *Metaphysics*,
and *De animalibus* on the feast of St. John the Baptist; *De celo et
mundo*, first book of *Meteorology* with the fourth, on Ascension
day; *De anima*, if read with the books on nature, on the feast of
the Ascension, if with the logical texts, on the feast of the Annunciation of the blessed Virgin; *De generatione* on the feast of
the Chair of St. Peter; *De causis* in seven weeks; *De sensu et
sensato* in six weeks; *De sompno et vigilia* in five weeks; *De plantis*
in five weeks; *De memoria et reminiscentia* in two weeks; *De
differentia spiritus et animae* in two weeks; *De morte et vita* in one
week. Moreover, if masters begin to read the said books at another time than the feast of St. Remy, they shall allow as much
time for lecturing on them as is indicated above. Moreover, each
of the said texts, if read by itself, not with another text, can be
finished in half the time of lecturing assigned above. It will not be
permitted anyone to finish the said texts in less time, but anyone
may take more time. Moreover, if anyone reads some portion of a
text, so that he does not wish, or is unable, to complete the whole
of it, he shall read that portion in a corresponding amount of time.

RULES FOR DETERMINATIONS
IN ARTS, 1252

STATUTES OF THE ARTISTS OF THE ENGLISH
NATION CONCERNING BACHELORS OF ARTS
WHO ARE TO DETERMINE DURING LENT

Chartularium universitatis Parisiensis, I,
227–30.

In the year since the Incarnation, 1251, the masters of the English nation, teaching in arts at Paris and for the good of the university and of learning taking multifold measures, and by God's grace continuing in the future without diminution, decreed by their common counsel and that of good men the form noted below for bachelors in arts determining in Lent, as is the custom. In the first place the proctor, touching the Bible, shall select two persons whom he believes qualified to choose examiners of those determining, who, touching the Bible, shall swear that without hate or love of any person or any part of their nation, they will choose three masters, whom they know to be strict and qualified in examining faithfully, more intent on the promotion and advantage of the

[1] Reprinted with permission from Lynn Thorndike, *University Records and Life in the Middle Ages* (New York: Columbia University Press, 1944), pp. 52–56.

university, less susceptible to prayer or bribe. These three when chosen shall similarly swear on the Bible that they will faithfully examine and proceed with rigor of examination, licentiating the worthy and conducting themselves without hate of any person or group of their nation, also without envy or any rancor of mind or other sinister perturbation. Moreover, those who have insufficient standing in the examination and are unworthy to pass they shall fail, sparing no one, moved neither by prayer nor bribe nor fear nor love or any other occasion or indirect favor of persons.

The masters presenting candidates, moreover, and the bachelors themselves shall give personal security that they will make no entreaties on behalf of bachelors nor seek favor from the examiners or from the nation or from the university, either by themselves or through others, but will accept the simple statement of the examiners. By the same token, if it happens that bachelors are failed, that they will not bring contumely or complaints or threats or other evils against the examiners, either by themselves or through others, because they ought to suppose that the examiners have acted according to their consciences and good faith for the honor of the university and the nation.

Moreover, a bachelor coming up for the licentiate in arts at Paris should be twenty years old or at least in his twentieth year, and of honorable life and laudable conversation. He should not have a cope without a hood of the same cloth, nor a hood with knots. He should not wear a mitre on his head in the classrooms while he is determining. If he has the right to the tonsure, he may have the tonsure, nor may he or should he be blamed on this account. Also before he is admitted to examination he shall give personal security that he has his own classroom of a master qualified to teach in it throughout Lent, and has his own master under whom he seeks the license of determining, or a bachelor about to incept in arts at the latest before Lent, in whose classroom he will determine. Further, that he has attended lectures in arts for five years or four at least at Paris continuously or elsewhere in a university of arts. Further, that he has heard the books of Aristotle on the Old Logic, namely, the *Praedicamenta* and *Periarmeniae* at least twice in ordinary lectures and once cursorily, the *Six principles* at least once in ordinary lectures and once cursorily, the three first books of the *Topics* and the *Divisions* once in ordinary lectures or at least cursorily, the *Topics* of Aristotle and *Elenchi* twice in ordinary lectures and once at least cursorily or if not cursorily at least thrice in ordinary, the *Prior Analytics* once in ordinary lectures and once cursorily, or, if he is now attending, so that he has heard at least half before Lent and is to continue, the *Posterior Analytics* once in ordinary lectures completely. Also that he shall have heard *Priscian minor* (books 17–18) and the *Barbarismus* twice in ordinary lectures and at least once cursorily, *Priscian major* (books 1–16) once cursorily. Also he shall have heard *De anima* once or be hearing it as aforesaid. Also he shall give satisfaction that he has diligently attended the disputations of masters in a recognized university for two years and for the same length of time has answered as required concerning sophisms in class. Also he shall promise that he will respond to question for a full year from the beginning of one Lent to the beginning of the next.

If, moreover, a bachelor shall be found sufficiently qualified in knowledge according to the examiners and shall not have completed the required number of years or books or lectures, the nation reserves to itself the power to dispense with these, as shall seem expedient to it. And in such case only it shall be permissible for his master to petition the nation for him.

Also if, after the exercise of cursory lectures has been made and finally completed, he shall have transgressed in the said exercise in any way, he shall in no case be admitted to the examination for determination. Nor similarly shall a master, whether now teaching or not, who, after the said exercise has been made as stated and finally confirmed by the masters, shall have transgressed in the said exercise, be accepted as presenting a bachelor, until full satisfaction shall have been made to the rector or proctors for the university by the master or the bachelor who has transgressed.

Also the bachelor licensed to determine shall begin to determine at the latest on the next day after Brandons. If he shall not have begun to determine then, he shall not be allowed to do so during Lent. And from the said Monday he shall determine continuously till the middle of Lent, unless he shall have lawful cause excusing him. And then let it be licit for no one to determine for him as substitute, unless such substitute has the license to teach in arts at Paris or has determined elsewhere through Lent or is licensed to determine in that present Lent, always providing that the same shall have determined continuously from the said Monday following Brandons until the middle of Lent. Also if a bachelor shall have been licensed to determine in the arts at Paris in one year and from a legitimate cause shall have failed to determine in that Lent in which he was licensed, which sometimes happens, he may afterwards determine in some subsequent Lent, regularly however and as others do, but he shall not substitute for others unless he shall have first determined during Lent in a fixed place. Also, until he shall have paid for the university a sum such and so great as he offered for personal security, and another for the nation, he shall not be given license to determine. Also if at the latest he shall not have been licensed before the last Sunday before Lent, he shall not be admitted later that year to the examination for determination.

Also, it shall be enjoined on him that all through Lent, and thereafter so long as he shall belong to the faculty of arts as student or teacher, he shall obey the mandate of rector and proctor in lawful and honorable matters. Also he shall not give drinks except on the first day he begins to determine and the last, unless this is done

233

by the permission of the rector or the proctor of his nation, who can give him a dispensation in this regard as shall seem expedient to them, considering nevertheless the many factors about the determiners which are here involved.

Also, the examiners shall diligently collect from the bachelors the money to be paid to the university and nation and faithfully keep what is collected, and at the summons of the rector and proctors of the four nations deposit it at the day set in the common chest of the university of artists. Also the money received for the nation they shall deposit in the common chest before the Sunday after Ash Wednesday. Also none of the said examiners can by himself, without his associates deputed with him for determinations, license anyone or presume alone to examine.

Also, in addition to the aforesaid, after the candidates shall have been licensed, let them be present every Friday at the Vespers of the blessed Virgin and at Mass the Saturday following, until Palm Sunday, under the penalty by which masters are bound.

But inasmuch as by this form it is not right nor will be for rich or poor, noble or ignoble, to put it off later, if they do not appear to seek license of determining in the aforesaid manner, therefore, to notify them it is provided by the masters that the present form be twice announced in classes each year, so that the first time it shall be read in the classrooms of masters between Purification and Lent, and the other time between the feast of St. Remy and All Saints or thereabouts, when there shall be a general meeting. Moreover, individual masters shall be bound on their honor to observe this ordinance. Also, however, if anyone is found acting contrary to the said ordinance, he shall be suspended from lecturing for a month.

Document 6[1]

GETTING A DEGREE

Antonino, *Summa*, III, 5, 2, 2.

Wherefore, there is required a vigorous examination by some lecture or disputation in which he must answer arguments. And then he has to be approved or rejected by a ballot of the members of the college according as the majority vote. And by the chancellor or vice-chancellor of the university is given him license to receive the doctorate, either in theology or law or philosophy or medicine, and the power of occupying a chair, of lecturing in universities, disputing publicly, interpreting, glossing, and the like. Then the recipient of the degree, after making a brief speech in praise of the faculty, requests one of his promoters whom he names and who is present that the insignia of the doctorate may be given him. And that one rising, after commending the candidate's proficiency in the subject in which he is to receive the degree and commending the doctorate, gives him the insignia: namely, first a closed book that he may have that science close and familiar in mind and may keep it sealed from the unworthy and in such respects as it is not expedient to reveal. Second, he gives him an open book that he may teach others and make things plain. Third, he gives him a ring of espousal to that science. Fourth, a cap as a token of aureole or reward. Fifth, the kiss of peace.

[1] Reprinted with permission from Lynn Thorndike, *University Records and Life in the Middle Ages* (New York: Columbia University Press, 1944), p. 309.

INDEX

237